For Ruth & Bruce — fellow Tower Heights n — Mark Abbott

TOWER GROVE

BY MARK ABBOTT

WITH KERRI BONASCH

FOREWORD BY RON (JOHNNY RABBITT) ELZ

REEDY PRESS
St. Louis, Missouri

Reedy Press
PO Box 5131
St. Louis, MO 63139

Library of Congress Control Number: 2009936608

ISBN: 978-1-933370-79-8

Cover photo by Mark Scott Abeln

Please visit our website at www.reedypress.com.

Printed in the United States of America
09 10 11 12 13   5 4 3 2 1

CONTENTS

ACKNOWLEDGMENTS

Writing by definition is a solitary activity, but a book, however, is always a group effort. Although there are literally hundreds of people who have participated in my research over the last decade, there are several people I would like to thank in particular. The research librarians at the Missouri Historical Society and the St. Louis Public Library were always extremely helpful and supportive. Without their expertise this book would have been impossible.

I would also like to thank the staff of the St. Louis Building Department. They were incredibly tolerant of my being underfoot for most of a summer. I also would like to thank Nola in the Assessor's Office at the St. Louis City Hall. She was always gracious in teaching and re-teaching me how to trace property ownership. I also must thank my supervisor, Dr. Wayne Smith, academic vice president at Harris-Stowe State University, who gave me release time when I most needed it, and members of the "Porch Club" who read several chapter drafts. But I would especially like to thank Kerri Bonasch and Matt Heidenry at Reedy Press. It was both an honor and a pleasure to work with them. Both are true professionals and scholars.

—Mark Abbott

FOREWORD

I n the following pages, the astute authors lay it on the line
about the facts of life in the Tower Grove neighborhood and
how this area continues, despite difficult odds, to regenerate
when several other city sections of comparable age and once-sim-
ilar characteristics have declined or have been decimated. One of
the keys to the district's ability to retain many of its decades-old
unique features as well as to assimilate new concepts and direc-
tions is Grand Boulevard itself, which entrepreneur and filmmaker
Walter Gunn, a Tower Grove resident, described as being the spine
of the city. Without question, the *raison d'être* for the viability
of Tower Grove is neighboring Tower Grove Park and its neighbor,
the Missouri Botanical Garden. The foresighted and philanthropic
Henry Shaw gave us these glorious legacies when the neighborhood
we now call Tower Grove was primarily prairie and grazing fields.

As this carefully constructed book relates, the neighborhood has
had its share of ups and downs, and there are those who will attest
its overall best days were in the 1910s to the late 1940s. They may
be right, but that's not to say Tower Grove hasn't been without
vibrant periods since that time, including today. As we entered the
"modern" age, many residents, or potential residents, for myriad
reasons, not the least of which was white flight, took off for the
breezeways and attached garages of the ranch houses of near suburbia. City residential property values at mid-century were extremely weak, and thousands of homeowners were bent on selling
out while they could as they were frightened by such realities as
the demise of the once-magnificent Vandeventer Place and that
homes on streets such as Flora Place, Flora Court, Hawthorne
and Longfellow boulevards, the private places of the Central West
End, and the larger homes of Midtown were dropping to prices
often less than those of the Great Depression. A case in point was
an impeccable, three-story, ten room, two bath, Federal style circa
1914 mini-mansion on Flora Place that in August 1949 sold for
fifteen thousand dollars—the identical asking price in that year for
the Chatillon-DeMenil mansion.

During this period of up-to-date suburban home construction there were still hundreds of residential buildings east of Twelfth Street using outdoor toilets. In this time frame, serious rehabbing and restoration was mostly unheard of and years away from reaching nearby districts such Lafayette Square, Benton Park, and Soulard. Therefore, these areas were truly down on their luck with a common consensus that they would never be revived. In those years, a growing contingent of city planners across the nation stated that the only way to save our cities was to basically eradicate rundown and old districts and build anew. This concept, which many felt was justified, started in earnest subsequent to the U.S. Congress passing a 1949 Housing Act that included an Urban Renewal Program. Such a massive land clearance for a redevelopment project would soon occur here in the area that is now known as the Mill Creek Valley neighborhood—a district not far north of Tower Grove. These were some of the same confused folks that a scant few years later would insist that the Old Post Office downtown, between Eighth, Ninth, Olive, and Locust streets be razed and replaced with a glass and steel office building. This silliness was stopped, after a bitter battle, by an effort initiated by businessman Frank T. Hilliker who had been a Tower Grove resident at 4012 Wyoming Street.

As a person who has frequented the Tower Grove neighborhood for decades, I find myself doing mental "surveys" of the district based on my memories and knowledge of what has transpired there. You may want to do the same, as well as to make notes and take photographs. Those who come after us will appreciate it as they'll want to learn what Tower Grove was like when we entered the second decade of the twenty-first century. Unlike some other areas of the city, this neighborhood's street names have remained constant. Here are some examples: Grand Boulevard was so named by its developer Hiram W. Leffingwell in 1850 as he planned this to be the "grand" street of the city and nearly as long as Broadway. Juniata is named for a river in Pennsylvania, but one time city sign makers goofed and put up new street signs on Juniata that bore the name Juanita. Wyoming is an Iroquois name that also comes from Pennsylvania, and Utah was named for the Ute Indians. Since the Connecticut Life Insurance Company was the principal developer in subdividing the neighborhood, Connecticut is thus named for that company and indirectly for the state in which the firm was located; Hartford, likewise, is for the city in which the insurance company had its headquarters; and Humphrey was the first name of the insurance company's president—Humphrey H. Green.

Tower Grove is blessed with many fine trees, especially huge mature American sycamores, but there's a definite need for a "reforestation" program. Some interesting vistas of the area are available from the roof of the Dickmann Building, the top floor of Tower Grove Manor, formerly the Marmaduke apartments, on Grand at Magnolia, and best of all from the observation windows of the Compton Hill Reservoir water tower. A tour through Tower Grove's streets will quickly show which areas are in need of more trees and which are like the lushly landscaped two blocks of Utah Place with its pristine parkway. These wonderful blocks are almost identical in feel to the six blocks of the Shaw neighborhood's Flora Place. And the medians on Grand south of Arsenal are delightful additions, as are the numerous trees lining Morgan Ford from Arsenal to Utah. These plantings have softened that area, which is at last getting much needed developmental attention. And it's good to see that parking meters haven't been planted on Morgan Ford. An interesting side note is that the original name Morgan Ford has at long last replaced Morganford, which for whatever reason had been commonly used for years. The Velvet Freeze ice cream shop, Cook's market, and the Armo air-dome theatre (an air-dome was a walk-in open air theatre) are fading memories of Morgan Ford, but new businesses are opening at a rapid rate. On Grand the Ritz with its small balcony is missed, as is the Spudnut shop just to the south of the theatre (spud nuts are donuts made with potato dough), the Shangri-la Rice Bowl restaurant, which was originally the Rice Bowl Tea Garden, was the first Asian entity of the neighborhood—it's where the King & I is today. A Walgreen's, complete with a soda fountain serving such treats as phosphates and tuna salad sandwiches, was at the southwest corner of Grand and Arsenal, which is where the Arsenal theatre had been located. That theatre went dark when the talkies came in. The Dickmann Building was for many years renamed the Queens Work, as it was principally occupied by a group known as "The Eucharistic Crusade of Knights and Handmaidens of the Blessed Sacrament."

There are many more memories of Tower Grove that are kept alive, since so much of the housing and commercial stock remains intact, with exceptions such as the two blocks south of Arsenal on the east side of Grand where all the old buildings were razed, and the vast seldom-used parking lot that runs from the rear of the Commerce Bank to Arkansas Avenue. There are streets that need some TLC, as there are in any neighborhood, but my personal award for the block that seems most representative of the general Tower Grove neighborhood of the past is Connecticut between Gustine and Roger Place. You can almost hear the streetcar bells in the distance, see the men after work in their long-sleeved white shirts with necktie tightly tied as they read the afternoon *Star-Times* or *Post-Dispatch* on their front porch as the lady of the house, in her house-dress, sat on a porch swing cooling herself with a hand fan. There would be no noise from power lawn mowers, just the soft sound of the blades from push mowers; no drone of window air conditioners or central air conditioning compressors. But you might hear the flapping of clothes on the line from back yards. Kids would be playing step ball, hide and seek, or mille. There'd be ash pits behind the houses and peddlers sharpening knives and scissors or selling fresh strawberries from hand-pushed or horse-drawn carts going up and down the alleys that divide the blocks of Tower Grove. You might run into a hobo at the back door who came for a hand out, far fewer cars would be parked at the curb, and with the windows open you'd faintly hear shows such as Sky King, Captain Midnight, Jack Benny, Straight Arrow, or maybe newsman Lowell Thomas on the radio. The future seemed far away. But it never is.

—Ron (Johnny Rabbitt) Elz

Chapter 1
A BRIEF HISTORY

Recently, urban historians have been discovering what many city residents have known for some time—that not all inner-city neighborhoods fell into inexorable decline in the 1960s and 1970s. This is part of a familiar story that urban historians have told and retold until it has taken on the aura of Gospel. The story describes the city's rise and fall, beginning with a golden age in the 1910s and 1920s with a vibrant downtown and thriving neighborhoods. However, the Depression and World War II caused the city to stagnate, making it vulnerable to suburbanization in the postwar era. As the story proceeds, the city entered a freefall in the 1960s and 1970s as whites abandoned the city to low-income African Americans who did not have the resources or the capacity to adequately maintain it. For some cities, however, the story has a somewhat happy ending. Just as it appeared that the city was doomed to be the depository of the hopeless, legions of professional-class whites salvaged it from ruin and decay, making it poised to experience a new golden age. It makes for good reading, but the problem is that it is not true—at least not for many inner-city neighborhoods.

Some urban historians are realizing that the story is much more complicated than they first thought. While some neighborhoods were abandoned, others—even some that abutted those that had decayed—continued to exist pretty much like they always had. Like a marriage that has withstood the test of time, there were undoubtedly good years and bad, but like a long-lasting marriage, these neighborhoods remained relatively stable because they possessed a solid foundation. Maybe they were never the trendiest of addresses, but they possessed numerous traits that allowed them to adapt to changing times and circumstances. So while there might be ups and downs, these neighborhoods maintained their populations, preserved their housing stock, cherished their institutions, and supported their businesses.

This book is the story of such a neighborhood—Tower Grove

in south-central St. Louis. Tower Grove remains a stable community, while more fashionable neighborhoods have come and gone.
Perhaps an understanding of how Tower Grove has worked for
over a century will shed light on just what makes a successful
community.

The area now known as Tower Grove is roughly bounded by
Shenandoah on the north, Nebraska on the east, McDonald on the
south, and Morgan Ford on the west. Tower Grove, as discussed
in this book, consists of three contemporary neighborhoods, each
with its own neighborhood association and character: Tower Grove
East, Tower Grove Heights, and Oak Hill.

FRENCH DAYS

Most of Tower Grove was part of a common field laid out
by the French in the 1760s called *Prairie des Noyers*,
"Meadows of the Walnut Trees." Unlike the English col-
onists along the Atlantic Coast, the French settlers who founded St.
Louis still practiced the Medieval practice of farming as a group.
Prairie des Noyers was one of five common fields that the French
settlers laid out on the periphery of the village. It stretched from
just south of what is I-44 on the north to Chippewa on the south.
The early settlers used the French unit of forty arpents to establish the width of the common field, and these eastern and western borders became the eventual paths for Grand Boulevard on
the east and the *Rue Royale*, or Kingshighway, on the west. Early
St. Louisans, however, were more interested in the fur trade than
farming. As a result, early Tower Grove during the French period
was little more than a poorly tended field full of weeds.

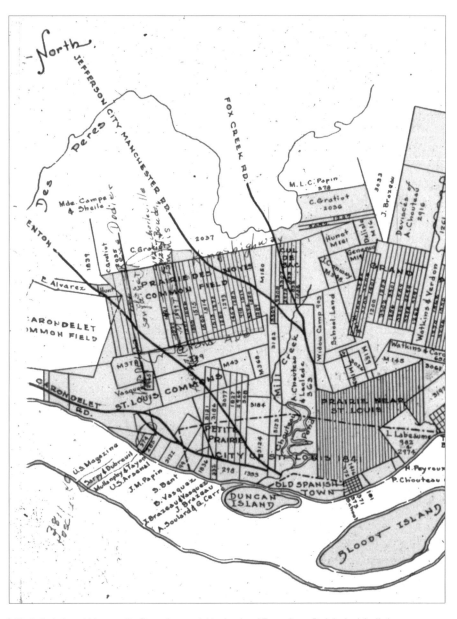

Most of what would become the Tower Grove neighborhood and Tower Grove Park had originally been part of the *Prairie des Noyers* (meadows of the walnut trees) common field that the French had laid out. However, what is now part of Tower Grove East was part of the old St. Louis Commons. The difference between a common field and a commons was that a common field was cultivated. Whereas, a common was pastureland used "in common" for livestock.

THE AMERICANIZATION OF TOWER GROVE

The Louisiana Purchase brought massive changes to St. Louis and Tower Grove. Not only did the Purchase accelerate the migration of Americans into the area, but it also introduced a whole new set of assumptions about property ownership and legal practices that would have a direct bearing on Tower Grove. The biggest change had to do with the common fields. Coming from an English legal tradition, the Americans had no way of conceptualizing joint ownership as was expressed by common fields like *Prairie des Noyers*. In some cases, the original French families confirmed their claims, but if not, the land reverted to public ownership. In either case, because of their proximity to the town of St. Louis, and hence their market value, the common fields were sold off to individual property owners relatively quickly after the American takeover.

A case in point was William Russell, who purchased 432 acres on the southern edge of *Prairie des Noyers* in 1805. The area that Russell bought is presently bounded by Gustine, Arsenal, Kingshighway, and Chippewa. Other major landholders of the early American period were the McDonald family and Robert Hunt, who owned major tracts between the Russell property and present-day Grand Boulevard south of Arsenal. By 1830, all of the land that would eventually become Tower Grove had been purchased by people with English surnames. The Americanization of the area was now complete.

While Henry Shaw stimulated a small amount of residential development to the north in what would become the Shaw neighborhood, Tower Grove was essentially rural until the last quarter of the nineteenth century, despite the fact that St. Louis was one of the fastest growing cities in the country before the Civil War. Between 1830 and 1860, the city literally doubled in population

George Ward Parker and the Parker Mansion at 3405 Oak Hill Avenue.

almost every five years. By the Civil War, St. Louis was the eighth largest city in the country, with a population of 160,000. Yet by 1860, the actual border of development was only out to Jefferson—about a mile east of Tower Grove.

Even if development from the city had stretched further, Tower Grove still would not have seen residential development at this time. Mill Creek ran just south of downtown and presented an almost impenetrable barrier between St. Louis and environs south—even after Chouteau's Pond, a small lake formed by damming the Mill Creek—was drained after the Cholera Epidemic of 1849. The valley created by the creek was almost like a moat that separated the city from the farmlands to the south. Broadway was virtually the only point of access that areas like Tower Grove had with the city.

The only real exception to Tower Grove's character as a farming community was Oak Hill—the name that William Russell had given his tract. Shortly after Russell bought Oak Hill, his brother James acquired the land and discovered a coal deposit near the present intersection of Morgan Ford and Tholozan. From 1820 until the deposits were exhausted in 1887, Russell and his descendants shipped coal in ox-drawn carts to St. Louis. Clay deposits

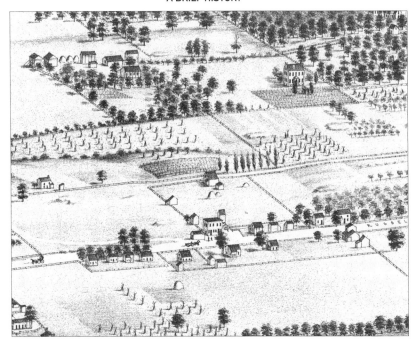

In 1876, the St. Louis firm of Compton and Dry published a *Pictorial St. Louis*. The atlas was a "bird's eye view" of the entire city comprised of seventy-five plates that depicted the city with incredible accuracy. The top plate is the land that became Tower Grove Heights. The bottom plate is a depiction of the new Tower Grove Park. The cartographers drew the city from the vantage point of a hot air balloon.

were also found in Oak Hill and became the basis of the brick industry in south St. Louis. The main company in the early days was the Parker-Russell Mining and Manufacturing Company (Russell's daughter, Russella, married George Ward Parker in 1854). The company's fire-brick plant was located near the present intersection of Morgan Ford and Parker.

Although Tower Grove remained primarily rural until the World's Fair, the nature of its residential development was determined shortly after the Civil War. East of Oak Hill, the McDonald property had been acquired by William Switzer, who used the property as collateral for a loan from Connecticut Life. Switzer died before the loan was paid off. Samuel Halliday was the executor of the estate, and he oversaw the transfer of the property in 1878 to the insurance company to cover the outstanding loan.

THE BIRTH OF A NEIGHBORHOOD

D efying the norm, Connecticut Life did not sell the property but tried to develop it. At first glance, it would appear that the life insurance company was a shrewd developer.

While the park is incredibly lush now, it was imposed on tree-less farmland. This is a view of the park from its northeast corner at Grand and Arsenal. Note the dirt streets.

The streetcar propelled the growth of South Grand between Arsenal and Utah. The poles that flanked the street carried electric lines and telephone wires. The automobiles are probably Ford Model Ts.

Tower Grove Park was established in 1869. Moreover, the city-county divorce placed the area squarely inside the city. No doubt they knew that the city planned to build a viaduct over Mill Creek Valley on Grand. The viaduct opened in 1882 and connected the South Side with the newly bustling Midtown area. The streetcar lines were heading toward Tower Grove from the east via Arsenal and Gravois, as well as from the north down Grand. Within ten years of acquiring its new property, Connecticut Life platted the new addition, Tower Grove Heights, in 1888, laying out the streets that would become the skeleton of the new neighborhood.

Even with the streets in place, development in the neighborhood began in fits and starts, with houses being built in a random, willy-nilly fashion. Despite a major recession in the mid-1890s that slowed down the country's economy, a great deal of building was taking place around Tower Grove. Compton Heights to the north was built out in the 1890s, as well as Shaw on the other side of the park. In addition, there was a great deal of activity taking place between Louisiana and Nebraska. However, by 1900, only a few houses had been built in the Heights.

Yet things were about to take a dramatic turn as three forces came together to cause the incredibly rapid build out of the neighborhood.

The first were the streetcars. By 1900, both the Grand line and the Arsenal line had made their way to the Heights. With the two lines intersecting at Grand and Arsenal, the intersection became a major transportation focal point on the South Side and would eventually make South Grand a major commercial center in the city.

The second major factor was that Connecticut Life decided it was not suited for the development business and swapped their undeveloped land for property in southern Missouri (literally swampland). The new group of investors was tied to the Mercantile Trust Company in St. Louis. The new company, called the Connecticut Realty Company, immediately began an aggressive marketing campaign. They also used their ties to the trust company to provide cheap financing to potential buyers. Mortgages, as people now know them, did not exist at the turn of the century. Loans were very short term—usually about three to five years—for only about 50 percent of the purchase price. The Mercantile loans were for greater amounts over longer periods of time.

The third factor in the Heights' rapid development was the 1904 World's Fair. The Fair had a palpable effect on business and residential development throughout St. Louis City. While there had been only a trickle of development between 1888 and 1905, the Heights was essentially intact by 1908. Once the Heights was built, the old Russell property to the west followed suit. Although it was not as organized as what had occurred in the Heights, the area that became known as Oak Hill was mostly built out before 1920.

THE GOLDEN AGE: 1910s AND 1920s

Connecticut Realty clearly meant for the development to attract a range of incomes. The deed restrictions dictated that some properties were to be single family while others were to be multifamily. None of the deed restrictions were fashioned in such a way to provide extremely exclusive housing or housing for

South Grand was a bustling place in the 1910s and 1920s. It had virtually everything that downtown St. Louis had, thanks in large part to the streetcars. Courtesy Library of Congress.

extremely poor St. Louisans, and the price points of the houses being built and the rents being charged for rental property made Tower Grove a community accessible for working people and professionals alike.

Tower Grove attracted both a wide income range and a wide variety of ethnic backgrounds. Census data from 1910 and 1920 show that Tower Grove had a large number of first- and second-generation German and Irish immigrants, as well as multi-generational residents who were of Anglo-Saxon descendent. While only 6 percent of St. Louisans were African American at the turn of the century, most of St. Louis—including Tower Grove—was off-limits to African Americans. In Tower Grove this was due mostly to tradition and social atmosphere. African Americans simply did not live in most parts of South St. Louis. However, unlike many parts of the North Side, the new subdivision regulations written by Connecticut Realty did not include deed restrictions that legally prohibited selling properties to African Americans.

If Tower Grove's residential institutional structure was mainly laid at the turn of the century and early 1910s, its business life came together during the late 1910s and throughout the 1920s. Grand between Wyoming and Arsenal quickly became the focal point of Tower Grove's commercial life. This is hardly surprising. Four streetcar lines served the Grand and Arsenal intersection. Today, commercial and office nodes are generally found where two or more freeways intersect. Before World War I, the key factor for determining business activity was where streetcar lines came together, because that was how most people got around before the mass production of the automobile.

By the mid-1920s, Grand must have been a sight to behold. While there had been a fairly large number of single-family homes on the street initially, those had been mostly forced out by the 1920s, replaced by two- and three-story buildings that generally had retail on the bottom floors and apartments above. Most of the businesses were oriented to the immediate neighborhood; however, there was a fair number, like the Omnimus Umbrella Company, that took advantage of the streetcar lines to serve a regional clientele. Grand had virtually anything that people could want. It had clothing stores, a "five and dime," music conservatories, and drugstores. What is now the CBGB bar housed an undertaker. The Dickmann Building, the largest on Grand, was built in 1926 and had one the largest concentrations of doctors and dentists in the city, although its office tenants varied. Lawyers, real estate agents, and various service groups all had their offices in the Dickmann.

Although not as busy as Grand, Morgan Ford still had its share of activity on the other side of the neighborhood. Because of the Arsenal streetcar, most of the businesses were close to the Arsenal intersection. But unlike Grand, Morgan Ford was not a regional destination. Most of the businesses served local needs.

Not all of Tower Grove's businesses, however, were located on Grand and Morgan Ford. Virtually every corner in the neighborhood had some type of small retail operation. Because few resi-

What is now the bar CBGBs (bottom) had been a funeral parlor (top). The neighborhood was first constructed just before Prohibition, and most properties on Grand had deed restrictions that prohibited from being "grog shops" or saloons. How times change!!

dents had cars (and even if they did, there was nothing comparable to the contemporary "supermarket"), they needed to walk to secure their daily necessities. As a result, most of these corner "mom and pop" stores tended to be food-related. Bakeries, small groceries, butchers, and the like dotted the neighborhood.

TOWER GROVE DURING THE DEPRESSION AND THE WAR

The Great Depression was one of the most traumatic events in American History. The economy shrank by a third as unemployment reached almost 25 percent. The Depression hit St. Louis particularly hard. Much of the city's economy was based around durable goods such as automobiles and steel. Because the purchase of those items could be delayed, durable goods firms suffered a great deal. Unemployment in St. Louis was over 40 percent for much of the early 1930s.

However, Tower Grove seems to have been relatively unscathed compared to the rest of the city. Orpheum Cleaners moved to their present location at Wyoming and Grand during the 1930s because their former Midtown location on North Grand had experienced a huge drop in business. Another piece of evidence that Tower Grove did not suffer as much as other areas of St. Louis is that St. Pius V undertook a major beautification project in the midst of the Depression. The church laid tile mosaics behind the altar—hardly an endeavor a church would undertake if it was financially strapped.

This is not to say that Tower Grove did not suffer during the Depression. Undoubtedly there were residents of the neighborhood who were either unemployed or underemployed. Although the *St. Louis Grand Gravois Booster*, a weekly newsletter published by the Grand Gravois Business Association, had virtually nothing to say about the Depression until 1931, it became a major topic thereafter. The newsletter told stories about struggling businesses and how the association started a "Buy and Deposit (a reference to the bank collapse of 1932) Campaign" in South St. Louis. There were also stories about the "United Relief Campaign" and the efforts of Mrs. Charles Alt on Hartford Avenue who was collecting old clothing for the "Welcome Inn."

Although Tower Grove may have suffered a little less during the Depression, World War II hit all segments of the city, including Tower Grove, equally hard. While it is difficult to determine how many Tower Grove residents were fatalities in the war, church bulletins and interviews with longtime residents suggest that the number was considerable. Many Tower Grove families would never be the same.

TOWER GROVE WEATHERS A STORM: THE POSTWAR ERA

When Tower Grove soldiers returned to their old neighborhood, things were pretty much as they had been before the war, but things were about to change. Tower Grove, like much of urban America, was about to experience the most traumatic period of its existence. For the next four decades, Tower Grove would be challenged by forces that were transforming America. The automobile, new governmental policies meant to stimulate home ownership, and the Civil Rights movement were coming together to fundamentally alter the American city.

Many neighborhoods across America—and in St. Louis—would not survive these changes. However, because of its many assets, Tower Grove weathered the storm. Maybe the most important of those assets was the diversity of its housing stock. Because many new suburban neighborhoods had larger homes with more amenities, many of the more affluent Tower Grove residents left the

neighborhood in the 1950s and early 1960s to live in trendy surbur-
ban communities.

So it is not surprising that streets like Hartford, Juniata, Halliday, and Crittenden, which primarily had impressive single-family
homes, experienced the effects of suburbanization first. Streets
like Connecticut, Wyoming, and Humphrey, which had more two-
family houses, generally fared better. A family could get a new
single-family house in a place like Affton or Mehlville, but multifamily homes in Tower Grove were still a better deal. As a result,
the heart of Tower Grove continued to thrive well into the 1970s.

The Grand Business District was another asset that permitted Tower Grove to weather the storm. Stores like *La Merite* Bridal Salon attracted brides-to-be from all over St. Louis. Grand also continued to
be a medical and professional center. It had restaurants and virtually
any retail or service opportunity that anyone might want or need.

Institutional life also remained a pillar for the neighborhood. Unlike other neighborhoods in the city—particularly on the North and
West Sides—the major churches in the area all stayed in Tower Grove
and did not relocate to the suburbs. Throughout the 1950s and 1960s,
churches in Tower Grove maintained their congregations. Parochial
schools up until the 1970s enrolled students at peak capacity.

Of course, another major strength of Tower Grove was the park
itself. It remained one of the most visited parks in the city. Although it retained its beauty, the many recreational areas of the
park were social centers for the neighborhoods that surrounded it.

So, while many neighborhoods in St. Louis experienced huge
declines in population and corresponding losses in housing stock,
businesses, and institutions in the postwar period, Tower Grove
remained relatively intact throughout the 1950s and early 1960s.
It still had roughly the same population as it had before the war.
It did not have large tracts of vacant houses. Moreover, Grand
remained a thriving business center. However, by the mid-1960s,
Tower Grove was showing some of the effects of suburbanization.

Virtually all of the housing stock was showing signs of disinvestment and disrepair. The community was definitely becoming poorer in relationship to not only the suburbs but also some other parts of the city. Most of the stores on Grand remained occupied, but they were not as prosperous. By 1980, Tower Grove institutions were beginning to show their age. Congregations shrank and the parochial schools experienced declining enrollments.

What happened? The bias of federal government housing programs like FHA toward single-family, suburban housing; the ease of freeway transportation; and the worsening condition of St. Louis public schools led to a decline in owner-occupancy and maintenance of rental property. Although it is hard to quantify, undoubtedly the controversy over school integration and busing remedies in the 1970s led to the flight of many longtime Tower Grove residents. The population remained fairly constant in these years, but the new residents tended to be poorer and lacked ties to existing institutions. Because many of these new residents came from rural areas in outstate Missouri and other parts of the upper South, they were usually not Catholic. As a result, the large Catholic churches and schools that had been mainstays of the neighborhood suffered in terms of both finances and membership.

The Tower Grove business districts remained healthy longer than the residential areas. While most of the mom-and-pop corner stores had died off due to the modern supermarket, Grand and Morgan Ford remained area attractions for some time due to the uniqueness of their stores. Eventually, however, suburban shopping malls offered everything that you could find on Grand for a cheaper price.

By the beginning of the 1980s, many urban pundits had written off Tower Grove and South St. Louis as just another inevitable casualty in the war between the city and the suburb. However, something surprising happened.

TOWER GROVE'S RENAISSANCE

The neighborhood started to show signs of resurgence in the early 1980s. While central cities across America and Europe had experienced similar phenomena in the late 1960s and throughout the 1970s, the neighborhoods that had gone through some type of resurgence were generally close to downtowns, college campuses, or nightlife districts. They were not in staid South St. Louis—the bastion of middle-class family life. Young, urban professionals (Yuppies) who were the vanguard of the "gentrification" movement were normally single and relatively affluent. They wanted—and could afford—an environment that was trendier than Tower Grove had ever been.

The "urban pioneers," however, who "re-discovered" Tower Grove in the 1980s were a different breed than the gentrifiers who had resurrected much of New York, Chicago, Boston, and even some sections of St. Louis like the Central West End. The typical new Tower Grove residents were in their late twenties to mid-thirties and just starting their families. They were teachers, nurses, or other lower income professionals, rather than the doctors, lawyers, and higher income professionals who gentrified other neighborhoods and cities. Tower Grove's attraction was its "un-trendiness." Although they wanted to live someplace that was more interesting than the suburbia of the 1950s and 1960s where many of them had grown up in, this new generation of Tower Grove residents were looking for a safe environment for their children, a lot of house for their money, and a place that had a strong sense of community. In short, they were looking for an alternative to both suburban life and the glitz of some gentrified neighborhoods.

The rebirth of Tower Grove occurred in almost the exact order of its decline. The streets with mostly single-family houses that were the first to slide in the postwar period were the first to recover. This was not all that surprising. Even though they had been

The Dickmann Building, circa 1980. Courtesy City Property Company.

neglected for some time, they were made of brick and/or masonry (which had been mandated by the Connecticut Realty Company in the initial deed restrictions) and withstood the test of time. Because they were built at the turn of the century, they had features not found in vastly more expensive homes in the suburbs: in-laid hardwood floors, crown molding, and tile roofs. Although some of these homes had extremely outdated kitchens and bathrooms, and some needed a great amount of interior cosmetic work, they could be tremendous deals for new homeowners willing or able to do much of the work themselves. Young couples, without much in the way of savings, were able to purchase much more home and much sooner than they would have been able to do so in the suburbs.

But there were problems. Tower Grove always had a reputation as being a safe neighborhood, and a trend of rising crime troubled newcomers and longtime residents alike. After a couple of sensational murders in the early 1990s, many residents panicked, especially since there seemed to be a rise in gang activity.

There were also challenges on Grand. For years, Grand had held up the neighborhood with its thriving business district. However, in the mid-1980s, it started to slip badly. A number of businesses had gone under, and they had either been replaced by lesser occupants or had become vacant. Woolworth's was a major loss in the early 1990s. The discount store had been a hub for decades.

Mounting class tension was another major problem in Tower Grove during the early years of its renaissance. Although most of the first wave of newcomers to Tower Grove were not extremely wealthy, they were considerably better off than many of the long-time residents—even those who were homeowners. Many of the newcomers had come to the neighborhood because of its historical character and wanted renovations to reflect historical standards, whereas older residents simply tried to maintain their homes any way they could. This was perceived by the newcomers as under-mining efforts to realize higher property values. In some parts of Tower Grove, there were tensions between homeowners and renters. By the 1990s, both homeowners and renters were attracted to the area because of its perceived value. However, because of differences in income and educational backgrounds, the two groups had opposing lifestyles that produced open hostilities since they often lived next door to one another. Sometimes this mounting class tension was expressed between sections in Tower Grove. The most overt tensions were between groups in the eastern section of the neighborhood—which increasingly claimed a separate identity as Tower Grove Heights—and the western section that had become known as Oak Hill. To highlight their resentment of what many of them perceived as patronizing attitudes of Heights residents, more than a few Oak Hill residents started to refer to their part of the neighborhood as "the Valley."

Another challenge that Tower Grove faced between 1990 and 2000 was its changing racial composition. The neighborhood experienced a dramatic increase in both its African American and Asian populations. The African American population jumped from 6 percent to 31 percent, and the Asian population went from 3 percent to 8 percent. This influx of non-whites produced some early tension between the groups involved. The tension, however, was much lower than anticipated. Many new African American and Asian residents were—like the whites who moved into the neighborhood in the 1980s—lower income professionals. As a result, they shared the same attitude and world-view.

For a number of reasons, by the end of the 1990s Tower Grove was in a position to experience a second wave of rejuvenation. One factor was a national real-estate boom at the beginning of the new millennium. In St. Louis, property values in the city rose faster than they did in suburban areas. As property values escalated, property owners and developers undertook riskier projects. Homeowners undertook major renovations. Developers, aided by creative state tax credits, purchased distressed multifamily apartment buildings and transformed them into condominiums. As the renovation fever accelerated, it gravitated to the western side of the neighborhood as well. Two-family units in Oak Hill were converted into larger single-family residents as property values increased.

Business conditions in the neighborhood also improved. Because of low rents and easy access, South Grand became a concentration of ethnic restaurants. The first restaurant was a Lebanese eatery called *Saleem's*. Although *Saleem's* eventually relocated to the Delmar Loop, it set the tone. As the Asian population in the area exploded, South Grand became a magnet for Asian restaurants—especially Vietnamese. By the end of the 1980s, South Grand was a regional destination point for people who wanted ethnic food. The success of the Vietnamese restaurants and the popular Thai restaurant *King and I* led to an influx of an array of ethnic restaurants coming to South Grand. At present, South Grand has everything from Afghan to Ethiopian. It even has an international grocery store.

South Grand has become a destination dining area that has acquired not only a metropolitan following, but a national one as well. South Grand features cuisines from every continent. It also has several groceries that have an international flavor.

Once a Kroger grocery store, Jay's International Foods now draws an international clientele from all over the St. Louis metro area. Customers from India, Cambodia, England, or Germany shop at Jay's to find that special taste of home. Country flags denote where the products of a particular country are found. It's a trip around the world without leaving the South Side.

Improved physical conditions also aided the resurgence of the South Grand business district. New construction filled in several unsightly holes, giving the strip a much more uniform appearance. The look of the district also was enhanced by the regular street and sidewalk cleaning provided by the new tax-supported commercial district. The increased prosperity of Tower Grove led to a flowering of businesses beyond South Grand. As prosperity moved east to west, business activity surged on Morgan Ford as well.

A third factor for the second Tower Grove renaissance was the continued strength of its institutional life. While the churches were not as strong as they once were, the fabric of community life remained strong. Tower Grove East, Tower Grove Heights, and Oak Hill each had strong neighborhood associations with regular monthly meetings, periodic newsletters, and active block units. When the neighborhood could have gone in either direction in the 1990s, the neighborhood associations faced the challenges of the neighborhood head on. They did not cause the real estate boom at the turn of the century, but they were instrumental in enabling the community to take advantage of the opportunity when it occurred.

Tower Grove Heights has had a neighborhood association since 1909. James Rollins, its first president, is pictured at the far left. He lived in the 3700 block of Juniata.

POSTSCRIPT

At present, Tower Grove is a neighborhood on an upswing, but neighborhoods, like any social organization, constantly face challenges. They either adapt and meet those challenges or they decline. Tower Grove is currently facing many potentially lethal challenges. The national housing crisis is threatening the neighborhood-wide rise in property values. There are still weak spots along Grand. Some storefronts remain vacant. There is too little retail. It is still too early to see if the turnaround on Morgan Ford can sustain itself. The racial character of the community may be the most tenuous challenge. In the past, racial diversification has been relatively tension-free. Another change to the racial character needs to follow this trend for the neighborhood to stay intact. Hopefully, those assets which have enabled Tower Grove to adapt in the past—a diversified housing stock, a strong business district, a thriving institutional life, and the park—will enable Tower Grove to meet those challenges as well.

The reflection pond in Tower Grove Park is one of the most restful spots in St. Louis. Courtesy Library of Congress.

Chapter 2

TOWER GROVE PARK

Tower Grove Park is the heart of the Tower Grove area. This is not all that surprising. Parks are often community focal points. But for this section of St. Louis, Tower Grove Park is not just its heart, it is its soul. The park is the force that transforms this collection of neighborhoods into a community. Throughout its history, "the" park has immersed rich and poor, native and immigrant, and black and white in a shared magical experience. Tower Grove Park has always been more than just a place to relax and recreate. It has been a place where folks from all the adjoining "sub-divisions" have put their conflicting backgrounds and interests on hold to stroll, picnic, and play together as neighbors.

Henry Shaw. Courtesy Tower Grove Park.

The park opened in 1872, but its story begins much earlier. Even before 1867, when Henry Shaw donated a portion of his estate to the city of St. Louis to become parkland, the vision of a park in St. Louis had been brewing for at least a century. Throughout most of civilization, few cities have created parks. Though most ancient and classical cities and towns had public spaces, these spaces were

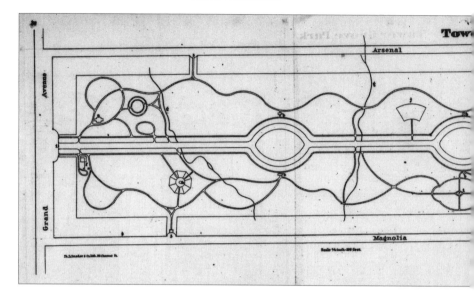

Henry Shaw designed Tower Grove as a "driving park." He envisioned visitors experiencing the park from the comfort of a carriage seat that would take the better part of a day. Courtesy Library of Congress.

devoted to commercial, political, and religious purposes. They were the places where city people traded, gathered as citizens, or prayed, but they were not the places where they went to recreate or to relax. Because cities were limited in size to the area that people could comfortably traverse by foot, if city people wanted to find a place to be alone or experience nature they merely had to walk beyond the borders of the city to find it. However, cities on both sides of the Atlantic started to grow beyond their "walking city" walls during the eighteenth and early nineteenth centuries. With early industrialization came the need to house more people and to form specialized places for trade and manufacturing. Omnibuses (large stagecoaches) and later streetcars allowed the city to stretch beyond its traditional boundaries and well into the areas where people could formerly escape the increasing noise and congestion of the expanding city. Europeans and Americans alike searched for remedies to counter what were then perceived to be the debilitating effects of urban life.

For many social commentators of this new urban-industrial lifestyle, the lack of nature was not only physically unhealthy, but also emotionally and psychologically, particularly for the new

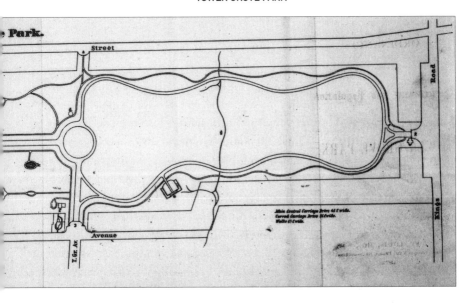

working classes. In their minds, open space was necessary not only to cleanse the air of disease-causing elements, but also to calm the urbanite from the hubbub of contemporary urban life. The rich and the middle class could escape to the countryside by carriage, but the poor and the wage workers were stuck in crowded tenements, factories, and city streets. Without relief, the poor would die from diseases like cholera (which struck the city with deadly force in 1849) and—in the middle- and upper-class mind, at least—become more agitated and unruly.

What is surprising about the early park movement—considering that its major rationale was physical and mental health—is that its initial impetus was a corresponding movement to bury the urban dead in cemeteries. Up until the nineteenth century, most dead on both sides of the Atlantic were buried on church property. However, as cities grew larger, this was simply not acceptable due to health reasons. The decaying bodies would leach into wells, polluting drinking water. Consequently, the practice of burying the dead in dedicated cemeteries on the periphery of the town or city gradually became the norm.

These new cemeteries, however, increasingly were seen not just as the domains of the dead, but also of the living. As cities became more congested with early industrialization, these peripheral burial grounds were perceived as potential open spaces that would provide ideal venues for quiet meditation and contemplation. Cemeteries, like Mount Auburn in Cambridge, Massachusetts—located just outside of Boston—became the model of what cemeteries could offer the living. Founded in 1831, Mount Auburn treated the visitor to carefully landscaped grounds and stunning architecture meant to inspire and sooth the living, not the dead. When the deadly cholera came to St. Louis in 1849, killing one-tenth of its inhabitants, the city followed Boston and other eastern cities' lead by building Bellefontaine and Calvary cemeteries on the north side with their spectacular terrains and views of the Mississippi.

Not surprisingly, urbanites soon wanted their own park space that they would not have to share with the dead. Although American cities, like those in Europe, had always had small public spaces, by mid-century, American cities were following Europe in constructing parks on the outskirts of the city expressly for relaxation. It is this impetus that led Henry Shaw to create Tower Grove Park.

Tower Grove Park was not Shaw's first project in St. Louis. Shaw had come to St. Louis from England in his teens and quickly made a fortune in the hardware business. When he retired in 1840 at the age of forty, his thoughts turned to travel, especially to his native England. Once in England, he was awestruck by the botanical gardens that many English gentry had created to study horticulture, and he was determined to duplicate such a project around his St. Louis villa, Tower Grove. Of course, this project was the foundation for the Missouri Botanical Garden, which opened in 1859.

However, the purpose of a garden—especially a botanical garden—was different than that of a park. From the very beginning, Shaw's goal in creating the garden was to promote the science and the study of botany. While the garden was always meant to be open to the public, its public function was to education and elevation—not relaxation. So, almost immediately after he opened his garden to St. Louis, Shaw began planning his next endeavor—an

The park has been a favorite destination for generations of St. Louis picnickers. Courtesy Tower Grove Park.

"ornamental pleasure ground"—that he intended to be grander than any other city park in America.

The foundation of this endeavor was a "deal" that Shaw made with the city of St. Louis. Shaw would donate three hundred acres of his personal estate to the city for a park. In exchange, the city would pay for improvements and annual maintenance. In addition, the city would relinquish control of the park to a Board of Commissioners that would be appointed personally by Shaw and after his death by the Missouri Botanical Garden. No wonder that Shaw was able to retire at forty; it was a hard bargain. While the land was worth over $300,000 in 1866 (equivalent to roughly $1.2 to $1.5 million in today's dollars, although today the land can be argued as priceless)—hardly an offer that the city could easily refuse—Shaw got the city to "pony up" an even larger amount for making the land into a park ($360,000) and agreeing to maintain the park in perpetuity. However, the real heart of the deal, and what has enabled the park to remain one of the premier parks in the country, was Shaw's demand that the park have a separate administration from that of the city. While the city footed the bills, Shaw and the

Board of Commissioners controlled—and continue to control—park operations. As a result, the park has never had to rely on the vagaries of the city or the Parks Department.

The other novelty of Tower Grove Park is that Shaw attempted to replicate a European practice of surrounding public parkland with private estates. Shaw envisioned a park encased inside a ring of villas situated on a two-hundred-feet-wide strip of land circling the park. But this strip would not be turned over to private ownership; instead, the owners of the villas would own the structure, but would lease the land that they sat on. This arrangement would achieve two goals. One, it would insure that the land would be used as intended. Two, because Shaw assumed that the wealthy would flock to live next to a gorgeous landscape, rents from the land would be high and generate a substantial amount of revenue. Interestingly though, monies were not meant for the park, but for the Missouri Botanical Garden. Though Shaw's idea for the strip never caught on (only one villa was built as intended), it was a fortuitous part of Shaw's plan, because the land ultimately reverted to the park and allowed it to incorporate new uses over time as they came into vogue.

But what has made Tower Grove Park so special since 1872 has not been its unique administration or novel land use ideas. Rather, it has been Shaw's brilliant plan for the park. Unlike most parks of the period, Shaw did not intend Tower Grove to be a "walking park," but a "driving park." As he envisioned it, city residents would drive their carriages out to the park (at the time, most of it was just outside of St. Louis's city limits) and would slowly traverse the park's meandering oblong roadway through a variety of wooded areas. Undoubtedly, Shaw assumed that a trip through the park would be an all-day affair. Not only was the drive more than three miles in length, but Shaw also meant for park goers to exit their carriages and roam the spacious grounds by foot on a network of walkways to admire the park's botanical wonders. It was an experience to be savored slowly so that park goers would receive the full benefit of nature's healing powers.

However, Shaw did not mean for this experience of nature to be unstructured. While Olmsted and Vaux attempted to make Central Park in New York as close as possible to a true natural environment utilizing a landscape style called "picturesque," Shaw never shared such a vision. The park that he envisioned would be more of a work of art than a work of nature. For Shaw, a park, like a garden, was not to replicate nature but to improve it. The "gardenesque" style Shaw espoused saw the park planner or gardener "creating" beauty through a series of landscape scenes that were comparatively small and possessed smoothness—not the rough edges of true nature. This "cultivated style" that Shaw pursued implied order and systematic arrangement where the gardener showcased nature. On the other hand, Shaw was not after some contrived or artificial conception of nature like the geometric patterns of the gardens at Versailles. Shaw sought a middle ground between formalism and the picturesque, where the controlling principle was harmony between art and nature.

Once Shaw had gained the city's approval to move forward with park plans in 1868, he began the work of constructing the park with his chief assistant, Francis Tunica. While the two later apparently had a falling out, Tunica had worked with Shaw at the garden and would be his chief lieutenant in carrying out the park plan. An engineer and architect, Tunica worked with Shaw to carefully lay out the park infrastructure with its roads, bridges, walkways, pavilions, and gateways. The plan called for ten bridges; thirty-five thousand feet of macadamized walkways, and seven miles of roadway, much of which was lined with stone guttering. In addition to the circulation system, the plan called for four major entrances and numerous pedestrian gateways.

Architecturally, the two most noteworthy features of the park plan were the entrances and the park pavilions. Each of the entrances had a unique design. The west entrance on Kingshighway featured forty-foot-high stone towers. The north entrance off Magnolia was characterized by fifteen-foot columns topped with

North gate, Magnolia Avenue, 1880s. The park superintendent's house sits just east of the entrance. Courtesy Tower Grove Park.

limestone spheres, which had been taken from the Old Courthouse when it was remodeled. The south entrance had eight pilasters or squared off columns that were connected with wrought iron. However, the most impressive of the four entrances was the eastern one that faced Grand Boulevard toward the city of St. Louis. This entrance featured both griffins, a mythological cross between a lion and an eagle that symbolized vigilance, and weeping lions, which were copied from Pope Clement XIII's tomb in St. Peter's Basilica in Rome. Not only was each of the gates themselves distinctive, but each of the gates had accompanying unique gatehouses. These were the residences of the gatekeepers who locked the gates each night. (The gatehouses have all been demolished except for the one on Arsenal, which is now used for children's art programming).

But the architectural feature that captured the attention of early park goers—and which continues to capture the attention of present-day park goers—were the pavilions. Twelve in number, these summerhouses were designed with a mixing of architectural styles that was popular in the nineteenth century. The summerhouses, which were meant to shelter picnickers, exhibited Romanesque, Gothic, Turkish—even Chinese—elements. As one student of the

Grand Boulevard Entrance. Courtesy Tower Grove Park.

park, NiNi Harris, has observed, the gazebos created a "fairytale atmosphere" that was "light, playful, even amusing." But not all aspects of the gazebos were amusing. The largest gazebo—the Turkish Pavilion, which is just east of the center roundabout— originally had a dove-cote for pigeons to roost above the picnickers, presumably so that the picnickers would be soothed by the cooing of the birds. However, shortly after Shaw's death, the park commissioners decided that picnickers and pigeons did not go together and covered the entrance to the dove-cote in 1892.

Although not one of the summerhouses, the Music Stand was part of the original plan. Located in close proximity to the Turkish Pavilion east of the center circle, the Music Stand was intended to be a vehicle for exposing all St. Louisians to "light classical music." Beginning in 1873, Shaw paid for park goers to hear compositions by his favorite composers: Mozart, Rossini, Wagner, Beethoven, Gounod, and Verdi. In addition to paying for these free public concerts, Shaw also commissioned the casting of bronze busts of each of these composers so that the concert goers would be inspired by their images. Each of the busts was placed on top of a polished red granite pedestal that lined a pathway circling the

One reason for the park's national reputation are the fascinating picnic pavilions. Courtesy Library of Congress.

One of the favorite things to do on a hot summer St. Louis night for over a hundred years has been to listen to music in the park. Courtesy Tower Grove Park.

bandstand. While Shaw installed eight pedestals, he died before he could commission the castings of Sir Arthur Sullivan and Ross C. Adams—two more of his favorite composers. As a result, two pedestals feature only marble spheres. (Due to weather, pollution, and vandalism, the original busts had badly deteriorated by the 1990s and have been recast.)

Two other major design features were added to the park after it opened but before Shaw's death in 1889: three major statues and a pond with fountain and ruins. Each of the three twenty-foot statues were composed by a German sculptor, Baron Von Mueller of Munich. The first one commissioned was of William Shakespeare and was situated inside the Center Drive roundabout. The only one that faces east, it was unveiled on April 23, 1878, the 314th birthday of the great playwright. Like the other statues, the Shakespearean statue is situated on a masonry base that has bronze bas-reliefs on each side. The bas-reliefs below the image of Shakespeare depict scenes from Shaw's favorite Shakespearean plays. There are images of Falstaff, Hamlet and the grave digger, Lady Macbeth, and Queen Katharine. The second statue unveiled was of Alexander Von Humboldt, the famous nineteenth-century philosopher and scientific explorer; it was placed to the east of Shakespeare near the labyrinth evergreen maze. Though little recognized at present, Humboldt represented the essence of Shaw's vision for both the garden and the park. They both were meant to inspire and educate St. Louisans—rich and poor—about the wonders of nature, particularly those of botany and horticulture. The statue, however, that was the most controversial was that of Columbus, which was located just inside the Grand entrance. Apparently, Shaw and Von Mueller had a heated controversy concerning whether Columbus should be depicted with a beard. Von Mueller said no. Shaw said yes. (Interestingly, Shaw did not have a beard.) Since money talks, Tower Grove Park is one of the few places in the world where there is an image of Columbus with a beard.

The other design element that was added to the park relatively

The park has been a safe area for youth to explore since its inception. Courtesy Tower Grove Park.

early was a small pond located just to the east of the Center Circle. Ponds with fountains were common features of Victorian parks, but this was not possible until the water lines were extended past the park to the Asylum for the Insane on Arsenal. Once water was available, a small oblong sailboat pond was constructed with a water fountain in the middle. The pond was also distinguished by a "rockery" on one side. This rockery was an artistic arrangement of stone blocks and columns taken from the remains of the first Lindell Hotel, which was destroyed by fire in 1867. Originally, the oblong pond was grass on three sides, but a balustrade railing was added in 1899.

For Shaw, however, the key design elements were the trees and shrubbery rather than the architectural features. On an essentially treeless landscape Shaw planted nearly ten thousand trees that represented virtually every evergreen and deciduous tree that could be grown in Missouri's temperate climate. Shaw brought in trees from across North America, Northern Europe, Siberia, China, and Japan. Once he obtained his trees, Shaw and his staff did not plant them in a willy-nilly fashion nor like a "wild woods." He carefully arranged them so that each tree could be inspected individually and so that the trees could provide an uninterrupted view of the park's landscape. Shaw also paid close attention to the seasons. Gingkoes were planted for fall foliage. Evergreens were strewn across the park to provide color during winter months. Magnolias and flowering trees were clustered to supply spectacular views in the spring.

While the park is now noted for its use of flowers and its lily ponds, Shaw—even though he loved roses—did not believe that flowers conformed to the gardenesque vision. So while Shaw did display some exotic plants that he grew in his Palm House or greenhouse, he did not plant large flower beds in the park. The prominent use of flowers in the park did not come until after Shaw's death when James Gurney, Shaw's chief gardener, became the park superintendent.

James Gurney, the park's first superintendent, never tired of standing on his beloved lily pads for photographers. Courtesy Tower Grove Park.

The meadows on the western end of the park were intended as points of contrast to the wooded areas. Courtesy Tower Grove Park.

Because the park was beyond the line of settlement in the early years, it had relatively sparse attendance compared to today. The surrounding neighborhoods and the streetcars were a quarter century into the future. Nevertheless, it was amazing how large park attendance was, given how far away it was for most St. Louisans. Six years after the park opened, Shaw recorded that 1,741 people visited the park on a Sunday in June. Not surprisingly, the majority came by carriage. On that Sunday, 683 carriages entered the park with another 15 saddle horses. Yet even though dense residential areas were a mile away, there were 401 pedestrians that day.

Since 1878, annual park attendance has grown into the millions. The reason it has continued to be so popular even after a century is that while the design of the park has remained sacrosanct, the use of the park has evolved to meet the needs and interests of the amazingly diverse array of people who use it.

The first major change in park usage came shortly after the turn of the century with the introduction of athletic fields. The

The playground has always been a favorite area in the park for Tower Grove kids and their parents. At top, the playground in the 1920s; at bottom in 2008. Courtesy Tower Grove Park.

original park movement of the mid-nineteenth century envisioned parks as quiet, restful places that were intended for meditation, not exercise. But as Americans became more urban and started living more sedentary lives, many city dwellers sought venues for physical activity—especially for their children. While the park commissioners (many of whom came from a genteel background) initially fought this trend, they grudgingly came to accept it and gradually introduced recreational facilities and activities into park life. The first activities to be introduced were the middle-class pursuits of tennis and golf. Tennis was played on both grass and clay courts; the small golf course was the first co-ed course in the area, started in 1903. These were quiet games that conformed easily into the park landscape. Also introduced early in the twentieth century was a playground with an adjoining wading pool, both intended for small children. Today, the sport of fashion is kickball, featuring teams with uniforms, team banners, and tailgate gatherings.

The park has always adapted itself to changing fashions in recreation. The park's tennis courts have long been a private club to neighborhood members. Courtesy Tower Grove Park.

Kickball is the latest craze in the park. Most leagues are coed. Sometimes players dress-up, not in uniforms, but costumes. Courtesy Tower Grove Park.

What the commissioners fought against for years was the introduction of ball fields. Baseball, football, and soccer—popular games by the twenties—would bring thousands of older, noisier children into the park, which would conflict with the park's desired use. As the commissioners wrote in a 1911 annual report, "the sports and games possible in a park of this character are limited chiefly to those in which children can safely engage, or those which do not affect the comfort of safety of persons pursuing other inclinations."

However, one senses that it was not just the noise that the commissioners feared. Ball fields would attract youth of a class lower than they were comfortable. Going back to Shaw, one of the functions of the park had always been to uplift the lower and working classes of St. Louis. As the commissioners argued in a 1922 report, "recreation in city parks means more now than ever before. The growing child requires special opportunities, if he is to develop in a citizen who can take place in the community . . . [recreation was important because it created] a spirit of fair play and sportsmanship and keener perception of the rights of playmates." Yet this was envisioned as taking place in a very structured, controlled atmosphere where the middle class could instill their values into those not as fortunate as themselves. But as the athletic fields were introduced after 1920, it was clear to the commissioners that the working class was not always interested in being inspired. Noting that athletic teams from other neighborhoods generally won competitions with neighborhood youth, the commissioners noted that "children in the less fortunate districts who are surrounded by the constant reminders of the sever[e] struggle for existence, give to their competitive play a more zestful character, a more vigorous determination to win."

Class tension was not the only social challenge that the park has had to overcome. Race has also been an issue. While the park never

The park's superintendents initially resisted baseball but later came to embrace it. Courtesy Tower Grove Park.

The splash pool draws hundreds of young kids on hot summer days. The pool has had many incarnations, but it has always been a big hit. Pictures from the 1920s are above. Above right is an image of the fountain in the 1970s, and bottom right, in 2007. Courtesy Tower Grove Park.

One of the wonders of the park is that while it has maintained the integrity of its design, it has evolved to meet the needs of a wide range of groups and uses. The park has hosted PrideFest, the annual festival of the gay and lesbian communities, for years.

had a stated segregationist policy, for much of the twentieth century, it was implicitly understood that the park was "off-limits" to St. Louis African Americans. As they migrated into St. Louis from the 1920s into the 1960s, African Americans instinctively realized that they were not welcomed in the park. Not only was it situated in the heart of highly segregated South St. Louis, but also it had the aura of being a private park that was open only to white St. Louisans. It would not be until the late 1970s when African Americans would feel comfortable in the park.

However, what is noteworthy is not that there have been class and race—and later, ethnic—tensions associated with the park, but that they have been as minimal as they have been. While the park had a reputation for vice in the late 1970s and early 1980s, it has never been seen as a high crime area. Even in the early 1990s when the surrounding neighborhoods were undergoing a period of relatively rapid demographic change and experiencing a higher than usual crime rate, the park was generally perceived as a safe haven. Throughout its history, it is as if people when they entered the park have "suspended" their class, racial, and ethnic hostilities and peacefully respected their fellow park goers' use of the public land. It is not uncommon to see white and black children in the playgrounds playing together with their parents talking to one another in the background. Nor is it uncommon to hear four or five different languages being spoken at the same time.

Tower Grove Park truly has been—and continues to be—a magical place. The park is thriving more than ever in the twenty-first century. Since the arrival of the current park superintendent, John Karel, in the mid-1980s, the park has become recognized as a national landmark. As the park has become more financially stable, it has worked to maintain the essence of the initial grandeur of Henry Shaw's masterpiece. But the real grandeur of Tower Grove Park is not the variety of trees, or the pavilions, or the ruins; it is what it has become and what it represents. Hosting everything from a Pagan Festival to PrideFest to the International Festival, the park epitomizes why Tower Grove is such a special community.

The Tower Grove Farmer's Market is a new use in the park that has become incredibly popular. It is now the place to be on Saturday mornings during the summer. Courtesy Tower Grove Park.

A NEIGHBORHOOD OF NEIGHBORHOODS

Aneighborhood is a concrete yet nebulous thing. While everyone knows that neighborhoods exist, virtually no one—including sociologists and urbanists—can agree on what a neighborhood actually is. Further complicating the issue, most people can give a name to their neighborhood and describe its boundaries, but it is not unusual to ask three different residents to name their neighborhood and get three different answers.

Capturing the essence of Tower Grove is especially difficult, because it is a neighborhood of neighborhoods. Different sections have vastly different identities, even though they all orient themselves toward Tower Grove Park. But this is Tower Grove's magic. Its pluralistic, overlapping web of identities gives the neighborhood its character and strength.

Like a natural habitat, a neighborhood needs both commonality and diversity to thrive. It needs common characteristics to hold it together and to give it a sense of place, as well as variety in terms of class, race, and architecture to make it interesting and capable of adapting to internal changes and external threats. While Tower Grove's diversity can sometimes lead to tension among residents, it is also the force that creates the synergies that pull them together into a community.

Although Tower Grove is a complex web of intertwined cultures and functions, for the purposes of our story, perhaps the best way of approaching the neighborhood is to describe it as a collection of three neighborhoods that have established rather discernible identities over time: Oak Hill, Tower Grove Heights, and Tower Grove East. What follows are thumbnail sketches of these mini-neighborhoods.

Oak Hill

Oak Hill is the mini-neighborhood that is the hardest to pin down. A jumble of building styles reflecting development that took place over a generation makes it difficult for residents to agree on the boundaries of Oak Hill, or even the community's actual name. The name "Oak Hill" dates back to 1889 when the Oak Hill Improvement Company subdivided a part of the original Russell tract, but probably just as many residents call their neighborhood Tower Grove South—the official city designation—even though this label refers to a much larger area. Undoubtedly, most residents of this part of Tower Grove perceive Gustine and Arsenal as the eastern and northern borders, respectively. However, the southern and western boundaries are harder to agree upon. While the city of St. Louis and the Grand Oak Hill Community Development Corporation—the defacto Oak Hill neighborhood association—have made Chippewa and Kingshighway the southern and western borders, most area residents see the community in more limited terms. Because the areas south of Humphrey and west of Morgan Ford have such different characters, most residents see the neighborhood's borders as Gustine on the east, Humphrey on the south, Morgan Ford on the west, and Arsenal on the north.

Oak Hill is both the oldest and youngest of the three mini-neighborhoods. Because of the coal mines, pockets of homes were built shortly after the Civil War. As a result, some of the homes were constructed even

The Grand Oak Hill Community Corporation.

before the city-county split of 1876. Most of these first homes were two-story frame houses that did not have to meet the stringent St. Louis fire codes that had evolved in the wake of the Great Fire of 1849. Also because it initially lay outside of the city, much of Oak Hill developed in a rather sporadic fashion. Small builders constructed houses one at a time on lots spread out over the neighborhood, using different styles, different heights, and even different street set-backs. For the most part, though, this first construction in Oak Hill took place in the southern half of the neighborhood closer to Humphrey. Due to disputes over the inheritance of the Russell estate closer to Arsenal, the northern section of Oak Hill was not developed until after 1908. Because this section was built out much faster than the area to the south, it acquired a more uniform appearance and is architecturally very similar to Tower Grove Heights, which was built roughly between 1905 and 1908.

However, all of Oak Hill—both old and new—has had a much different social character than either Tower Grove Heights or Tower Grove East. From the beginning, Oak Hill has been a working-class neighborhood. Lacking enclaves of exclusive housing like Utah Place or Crittenden Avenue, Oak Hill has never had the cache that Tower Grove Heights and Tower Grove East have enjoyed at various times. Yet, Oak Hill has always had a very stable reputation. With strong anchors like the park, Holy Family Parish, and Mann School, Oak Hill thrived even as the more prestigious areas to the east struggled. Consisting mostly of two-family building stock, Oak Hill for most of its history has been a community of owner-occupants. Even in economically tough times, these families had their renters to help them out. So as the owners of the larger single-family homes in the Heights and Tower Grove East moved to trendier addresses in the suburbs after the Depression and World War II, the families in Oak Hill continued on much as they always had. While the eastern parts of Tower Grove experienced crime waves in the 1980s and 1990s, Oak Hill never was inflicted to the same degree.

On the other hand, Oak Hill's plain persona has sometimes been a source of tension in the community. Lacking larger single-family homes, Oak Hill did not share equally in Tower Grove's early gentrification. As the eastern sections of the neighborhood became havens for young professional urban pioneers in the 1980s and 1990s, Oak Hill remained essentially working class. This resulted in a not very well disguised class antagonism. The more affluent, better educated young rehabbers east of Gustine sometimes tended to look down on the older residents of Oak Hill who lacked the resources to maintain their homes to the same degree. But the resentment was often mutual. Sometimes when asked where they lived—especially if by someone they knew lived in the eastern half of the community—Oak Hillers often said that they lived in the "valley," to differentiate themselves and their status from those who lived east in the "Heights." However, over the last decade this tension has receded to a degree. As Tower Grove housing prices have escalated, Oak Hill has also become a magnet for younger urban pioneers.

Tower Grove Heights

The mini-Tower Grove neighborhood with the clearest and most consistent identity is Tower Grove Heights. While Tower Grove East's and Oak Hill's geographies have fluctuated over time, the Heights boundaries have remained constant: Utah on the south, Gustine on the west, Arsenal on the north, and Grand on the east. Although not identical to its original boundaries, the clarity of the Heights' identity dates back to its early days as a subdivision. When the Connecticut Mutual Life Insurance Company originally platted the area, they called it Tower Grove Heights, and it has been called so ever since.

The other factor that has given the Heights its clear sense of identity is the fact that it was developed nearly as a single piece. While the beginnings of the Heights was built out in fits and starts between its original platting in 1888 and 1904, the World's Fair created such a hot building boom that virtually all of the housing built in what is now known as Tower Grove Heights was built between 1905 and 1908. Consequently, the Heights has a very uniform appearance. Not only did builders respond to styles and trends common to the time, but deed restrictions placed on the Heights by Connecticut Realty (the new developer) when it re-platted the neighborhood in 1905 required all residential structures to be constructed of brick or stone, two and half stories high,

Completed in 2007, 3501 Juniata is an historic replica. The original building was possibly used as a confectionary. The rehabber's intended use was as a single-family residence complete with corner entry and second-floor turret. It sold before completion.

and set back from the street at a uniform distance. But because the houses were built by several builders, they have just enough diversity to be architecturally interesting.

The last factor that has given the Heights its clear sense of identity has been its social make-up. Although Connecticut Realty set aside certain streets for single-family homes and other streets for two- and four-family structures, even the multifamily properties tended to be more substantial than those in abutting areas, and this has given it a higher class tone—for better or worse.

The Heights had its Golden Age in the 1910s and the 1920s. Though it was not as prestigious a community as the Central West End during the same period, Tower Grove Heights was a very prosperous neighborhood. The single-family streets—Hartford and Juniata—were populated by doctors, lawyers, and business executives. Arsenal, Connecticut, Wyoming, and Humphrey—the two-family streets—were home to well-off wage workers and small business owners, while Utah Place featured some of the most distinctive homes in St. Louis.

In the summer of 1905, the Connecticut Realty Company and the Mercantile Trust Company teamed up to take advantage of the post–World's Fair real estate boom. After extensive advertising, the two companies held massive auctions where potential buyers were taken in horse-drawn wagons from property to property to bid on houses that were tied to cheap financing.

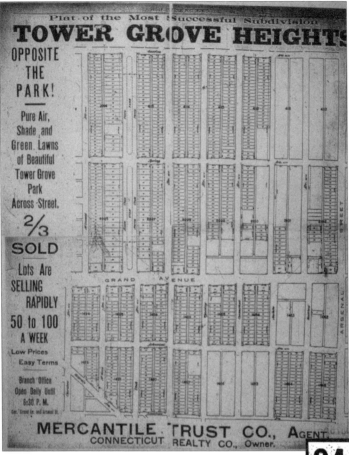

Map showing properties to be auctioned off. Blank areas were already built upon.

Like most of St. Louis, Tower Grove Heights suffered during the Depression and World War II, but the Heights fared better than most neighborhoods. However, during the postwar period the Heights lost much of its luster. Although the homes in the Heights—especially the single-family ones—were designed for members of the upper middle class, Tower Grove Heights houses did not have the spacious lawns and the newer amenities—like air conditioning—found in suburban homes. With the automobile and the construction of the new freeways, the Heights' streetcar lines no longer had the same appeal for upper-middle-income residents.

On the other hand, the interior streets consisting mostly of two-family houses remained quite stable. The large, two-family structures continued to be a good deal for working-class families—especially those who were just starting out. The rent from the second unit helped make the mortgage more affordable. Even when FHA and VA loans made it possible for many working-class families to have their own single-family homes in places like Affton and Mehlville, the Heights was still a better bargain throughout the 1950s and 1960s, especially for those families without cars. But by the 1970s, even the interior of the Heights was starting to look somewhat haggard. With the ubiquitous automobile and all areas of the city now affected by the school busing controversy, more affluent working-class residents on streets like Connecticut fled to the suburbs.

The Heights, however, started to recover in the mid-1980s. As with similar neighborhoods in St. Louis and across the country, the renaissance in the Heights first started on the single-family streets. Attracted by the ambience of the neighborhood and the architecture of the housing, young affluent professionals started to settle in the Heights, realizing that they could get more home for tens of thousands of dollars less than what they could afford in the suburbs. Generally in their late twenties or early thirties, these early urban pioneers were just starting their families and wanted a neighborhood where they could establish roots.

Rather quickly, Hartford, Juniata, and Utah became a haven for these young urban pioneers, who no longer saw "edgier" neighborhoods like Soulard or the Central West End as options. Yet they wanted an area that had more "spark" than the suburbs where many of them had grown up; they wanted a relatively safe neighborhood for their children, but a place that had appeal for them, as well. The Heights seemed like the perfect place. It had spacious Victorian houses, the stores and restaurants on Grand, and of course, the park. The only real drawback was the schools. By the late 1980s, St. Louis public schools had acquired a horrible reputation. In fact, the Secretary of Education at the time commented that St. Louis had the second-worst school system in the country—second only to Chicago. But with dual professional incomes, many of these urban pioneers could afford parochial or private schools.

The real attraction of the Heights for these urban pioneers was its sense of community. They were all about the same age, their kids played together, and they were all consumed by restoring their homes. In a very real sense, the Heights had come to define who they were. Their identity, in many cases, was one and the same with the neighborhood's.

However, as the Heights entered the twenty-first century, many of these urban pioneers found it hard to maintain the same level of commitment. With their children grown, their houses restored, and their careers evolving, this generation of Heights residents no longer saw themselves primarily in terms of their involvement in the neighborhood. While they were still captivated by the community's charm, these Heights residents—now in their fifties—no longer had the energy to devote to neighborhood affairs. Moreover, as the value of the single-family homes continued to escalate, new young couples who would have been able to restore much of this energy were unable to buy into the neighborhood.

But as in years past, the synergy between the single-family streets and those that are primarily multifamily continues to bolster the

Heights. Rising real estate values on the single-family streets ultimately led to a similar revival on the multifamily blocks. Though
this has not necessarily led to a revival of owner-occupancy in the
multitude of two-family dwellings, the interior of the Heights and
Arsenal have become magnets for college students and young professionals. As a result, the Heights continues to thrive as these new
residents become increasingly involved in neighborhood life.

Tower Grove East

Of Tower Grove's three mini-neighborhoods, Tower Grove
East has changed its identity the most over the years.
Once a part of the original Tower Grove Heights subdivision, Tower Grove East not only broke away to become its own
neighborhood, but it underwent drastic "personality" shifts over
the last four or five decades.

Tower Grove East was "born" as part of the William Switzer
estate that eventually became Connecticut Mutual's Tower Grove
Heights subdivision. As originally platted, the subdivision extended two blocks west and east of Grand. While the section west
of Grand would continue to be known as Tower Grove Heights,
the majority of the subdivision was actually in the eastern part.
Unlike the western part, which stopped on the north at Arsenal
because of the park, the eastern half extended four blocks north
of Arsenal to Magnolia. To the south, McDonald was the common
border of the subdivision.

In its early days, Tower Grove East between Magnolia and Arsenal was the "nice" part of Tower Grove Heights. Many of the houses
were built before 1905 and tended to be larger than those built during the post-Fair boom—especially those on Halliday and Pestalozzi. On the other hand, the section south of Arsenal developed in a
"hit-and-miss" fashion over a long period of time. Due to sink holes,
pre-existing nonresidential uses, a cemetery, and later Roosevelt

High School, this section of Tower Grove Heights never really fit in with either Tower Grove Heights or Tower Grove East.

By the 1920s, all of Tower Grove East was acquiring a unique identity apart from the rest of Tower Grove. Much of this was due to the filling in of development to the north and east. While a number of homes built in the 1890s north of the original Tower Grove Heights subdivision were rather substantial, they were nowhere near the size and grandeur of those in Compton Heights proper, which abutted this in-between section to the north. As a result, the residents tended to gravitate toward the Heights. The same was true of the area between Louisiana and Nebraska—only in an opposite direction. Never really part of a neighborhood, the area east of Nebraska was part of a general development that took place between 1880 and 1910 east of Jefferson as the streetcar lines expanded southeast. But for the most part, the housing stock west of Nebraska was more upscale than that east of Nebraska, which eventually became Fox Park. Consequently, residents in this other in-between land tended to associate with the more affluent section of Tower Grove Heights, which was now becoming known as Tower Grove East.

The other force that caused Tower Grove East to become more

This eclectic, full-service, 43,000-watt, listener-supported community radio station has been broadcasting in Tower Grove since 1987. Located in the former Barnabus Ficht Bakery, KDHX offers a full spectrum of music, which promotes local talent and provides a well-regarded forum for public discourse.

KDHX keeps its listeners informed on local cultural and public affairs and fosters education and community participation, which promotes and supports cultural diversity.

All music is hand-selected, with expert DJs showcasing both established and emerging artists. KDHX regularly features live in-studio performances and specialty programming dedicated to specific genres of music that you wouldn't hear anywhere else in St. Louis.

differentiated from the rest of Tower Grove was what was happening on Grand by the 1920s. South of Arsenal, the proximity of four major streetcar lines was transforming Grand into a retail and office center. But because the park occupied the western side of Grand between Arsenal and Magnolia, Grand Boulevard just north of Tower Grove Park took on an entirely different character. Instead of becoming retail and service oriented, this area became more directed to institutional, cultural, and entertainment uses. The Seventh District Police Station and Messiah Lutheran Church had located there shortly after the turn of the century. By the 1920s, the Alhambra Grotto, the Strassberger Music Conservatory, the Pelican Building (with its restaurants and night clubs), the Marmaduke Apartments, and a YMCA were all present on this northern section of South Grand, giving it a much different tenor from South Grand, south of Tower Grove Park.

Efforts to carve out a separate identity for Tower Grove East began in the 1920s with the erection of cast-iron signage. However, the community has always struggled to define who and what

When the neighborhood quickly developed after the turn of the century, it was necessary that the city of St. Louis provide services such as fire and police protection. The Seventh District Police Station was one of the first projects that the city undertook after the state amended the charter of the Metropolitan Police Department so that the city would have greater budgetary control over the department in 1899. The building permit was issued in 1900, and the building served the area between Compton and Kingshighway until 1960. Between 1960 and 1985, the building housed the National Association of Letter Carriers. In 1985, the building was renovated by the planning firm of WVP and was its corporate offices for several years. It is currently being renovated again as a condominium development.

it is. Unlike the Heights and Oak Hill, Tower Grove East does not possess a consistent architectural style or housing type. Individual streets—like Halliday and Crittenden Place—have very definite personalities, but the park is the only common thread holding the community together. Yet this disparate personality helped Tower Grove East remain stable during the postwar period. Not having as large a stock of single-family homes as the Heights and Oak Hill, Tower Grove East weathered the flight to the suburbs bettered than its neighbors to the west. However, by the 1980s, its diversity had become a weakness. Although some of its single-family streets experienced a resurgence in the 1980s and 1990s, the income disparity in the community led to social problems, including gangs and drug activity.

Located on Arsenal, the large and unique front entrance lantern adorning Riley's is hard to miss. This is another Tower Grove neighborhood landmark that has earned accolades from the *Riverfront Times*; Riley's has an intimate feel, a great selection of beers and whiskeys, and a fantastic jukebox that is definitely worth a look-see. Go Monday or Tuesday for St. Louis–style pizza specials.

The original structure built in 1895 was renovated in 2005. A Victorian tin ceiling was discovered during renovation. Riley's atmosphere is cozy with no frills, just nice people. The front booths are made from pocket doors; the Italian marble tables that were once windowsills add a nice touch. The staff is adept at recognizing the many regulars that come through. Riley's does not carry any AB products on tap—incredible for St. Louis!

Like the Heights and Oak Hill, though, Tower Grove East shared in the turn-of-the-century real estate boom, and its eclectic character again became one of its strengths. Having more large apartment buildings than either the Heights or Oak Hill, Tower Grove East has attracted a younger clientele than either of its sister Tower Grove neighborhoods, and it has an "edgier" identity. Small neighborhood bars and eateries have begun to attract patrons from all over the region as many single-family houses on the mixed streets have become the targets of a new wave of urban pioneers.

Grand Boulevard. Courtesy East-West Gateway Council of Governments.

Chapter 4

THE STREETS

P erhaps nothing defines a neighborhood's present—and past—as well as its streets. While most people think of streets as nothing more than carriers of cars, streets organize a neighborhood's terrain and give it a sense of place. They are where people meet and go shopping. On occasion, they are also political arenas and places of commemoration. For local historian Andrew Hurley, "streets ooze with history." As he explains, the materials of which they are made, the buildings that have lined them, and the businesses that have come and gone "all tell a story about the way life was lived in the past."

Tower Grove has great streets. It features everything from majestic thoroughfares to lively business districts, tree-canopied residential streets, and stately boulevards with architect-designed homes. These are the places where Tower Grove residents have traveled to work, ridden their bicycles, talked to their neighbors, and bought their daily bread. Because the community has such great streets and has come to be identified with them, it has even been named for its streets on occasion. What is now known as Tower Grove South used to be referred to by the city as Grand–Oak Hill. Even today, when many residents are asked where they live, they simply say "South Grand," knowing that everyone—at least everyone in St. Louis—will recognize where they live. Following are the stories of several streets that have shaped the life of Tower Grove.

Grand and Arsenal circa 1910 looking south. Shortly after this photograph was taken, the multifamily houses on the left were replaced by the Tower Grove Bank, which eventually became the present Commerce Bank branch. Courtesy Library of Congress.

GRAND

Next to the park itself, no other element defines Tower Grove as much as Grand Boulevard. Although it runs the length of the city, when most St. Louisans hear the words "Grand Boulevard," they think of Tower Grove's stretch from Arsenal on the north to Utah on the south. While other sections of Grand are important—like the Midtown section and its affiliation with Saint Louis University and the theatre district—it is "South Grand" and its collection of restaurants and shops that most people associate with this fabled St. Louis thoroughfare.

Although from the very beginning it was intended to be one of the most majestic boulevards in the United States, Grand was not always so grand. When it was laid out just before the Civil War, Grand was supposed to be a 120-foot-wide ribbon that would be the city's border for years to come. However, things do not always go according to plan. Grand was never as wide as envisioned, and it was the western border of the city less than fifteen years. With the city/county "divorce" of 1876, the western border of the city moved

The business district on South Grand has always served both neighborhood and regional needs. Though the balance has shifted over time, South Grand has remained a place where local residences can buy day-to-day needs like bread at the J.H. Waldeck Bakery (3201 South Grand at Wyoming), at top. At bottom, newsies prepare for their next customer, courtesy Library of Congress.

While local residents could buy everyday items on the strip, the streetcars brought retail shoppers from across the city to South Grand to clothiers like Wm H. Stamm's (above) at 3116 South Grand. Today, this is the home of the St. Louis Bread Company. However, the automobile and the advent of the shopping mall reduced the retail market share in neighborhood commercial strips like South Grand.

three miles to the west. But in the southern part of the city, Grand was little more than a rural dirt road until the turn of the century.

Things started to change rapidly, though, beginning in the 1890s. The first change was the arrival of the streetcar. By 1900, the neighborhood had two lines—one that came in from the east via Arsenal, and a second that came in from the north on Grand. Just like today, when commercial nodes spring up wherever two freeways cross, a commercial node emerged at Grand and Arsenal because of the crossing streetcar lines.

Even now, you can see how the development unfolded. With the streetcar lines crossing at Grand and Arsenal, the first commercial construction took place between Arsenal and Juniata. But south of Juniata, only the corner properties were built to be commercial. Over time, though, most of the original residential properties were replaced by shops and businesses.

The big transformation of the strip between Arsenal and Humphrey did not take place until the late 1910s and 1920s. By then, the streetcar had pushed development west of Kingshighway, mak-

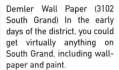
Demler Wall Paper (3102 South Grand) In the early days of the district, you could get virtually anything on South Grand, including wallpaper and paint.

ing Grand and Arsenal a central location. As such, buildings became larger and larger as the land became more and more valuable. By the 1920s, South Grand not only had large office buildings like the Dickmann Building but also large apartment buildings, like the one at Grand and Connecticut. However, more than the buildings were changing. While a few businesses serviced the immediate community, most targeted a citywide clientele. By the late 1920s, South Grand had numerous physicians' offices plus high-end men's and women's clothiers. Even during the Depression, South Grand thrived because of the streetcar lines and its central location. Orpheum Cleaners, for example, relocated to South Grand from North Grand near the Powell Hall in 1938 to take advantage of a stronger business district.

Throughout the 1940s and 1950s, South Grand was one of the region's most thriving business districts. The Butler Building (southwest corner of Arsenal and Grand) and the Dickmann Building were two of the most desired locations in the city for physicians and dentists. While there were a few bakers and barbers who served primarily a local clientele, most of the retailers—like furrier David Davis at 3161 South Grand (between Juniata and Connecticut)——served a much larger and fairly affluent market. However, that had started to change by the early 1960s. The flight of retail that

By the early 1980s, the strip was looking a "little long in the tooth." There were numerous vacancies, and it was attracting rather marginal restaurants and bars, as well as a second run theatre. The Rice Bowl is now the King and I, a regional destination restaurant that features Thai cuisine. The Ritz is now a public parking lot, just north of the King and I. Courtesy City Property Company.

accompanied suburbanization started to pockmark this once glorious strip. Though it was still the home of upscale stores like La Merite's Bridal Shop (Hartford and Grand), the strip probably had more vacancies than it had even during the Depression, and it was starting to attract tenants looking for class B and C office space. By the 1980s, just about all of the high-end uses had disappeared, and most of the office space was taken by nonprofits and marginal businesses. Instead of prestigious retail outlets, there were now cheap lounges and "greasy spoons"—like the Courtesy Sandwich Shop, later a hamburger place known as King's Way, at the northeast corner of Grand and Arsenal.

But by 1980, there were already signs of what South Grand's next life would look like. Though the cheap rents had attracted

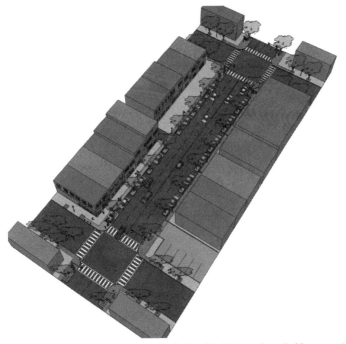

The Great Streets project administered by the East-West Gateway Council of Governments has allowed the South Grand Commercial District to bring in outside urban design specialists to develop streetscape and traffic flow plans to enhance the district. Recent federal allocations through the Economic Recovery Act should permit this vision to be realized. Courtesy East-West Gateway Council of Governments.

some not-so-desirable uses, South City's increasingly international communities made Grand a magnet for many of the ethnic restaurants and stores that would become South Grand's hallmark by the early 1990s. Saleem's Lebanese Restaurant, which would later relocate to the Delmar Loop, was initially located between Juniata and Connecticut. The China Bowl was across the street, just north of Juniata. Jay's Asian Grocery, which would become a mainstay of the strip by the 1990s as Jay's International Foods, started out in a small storefront between Humphrey and Utah. By the 1990s, numerous Vietnamese restaurants sat near eateries featuring Thai and Filipino cuisine. Eventually, the strip would also be the home to other French, Chinese, Thai, Afghan, Turkish, Nicaraguan, and Ethiopian restaurants.

This international flavor was the force that stimulated not only Grand's rejuvenation, but also that of the neighborhood. This mass of exotic stores and restaurants drew young people into the area, many of whom would later become the neighborhood's army of urban pioneers. As South Grand took on this "edgy" persona, it began catering to a younger clientele, spawning hip tattoo/piercing parlors, second-hand bookstores, and late-night hangouts. However, as the strip drew money into the district, it went from being edgy to trendy—attracting a somewhat older, but more affluent, market. By 2000, South Grand was drawing patrons from all over the region, which, in turn, has stimulated new development.

Although some people have lamented the passing of its more flamboyant phase, the newer development will probably prove more sustainable in the long run. The district's international flavor is perhaps more established than ever with such events as the annual International Festival, and South Grand has maintained its unique character as events like Pridefest have become institutionalized. At the time of this writing, South Grand seems to have acquired an ideal balance between young and middle aged that has something for all income groups. As the neighborhood enters its second century, South Grand is becoming one of the great streets in America.

MORGAN FORD

While the analogy can be stretched too far, neighborhoods are like living things. They are born, go through a period of maturation, have a peak phase, and are eventually transformed into something else. Like living things, neighborhoods and their streets also go through periods of health and illness. Sometimes they are thriving. Other times they are dysfunctional—almost as if they are diseased. And sometimes—just

An independently operated grocery store, Local Harvest offers local produce, meats, and organic foods, knowing that local food tastes fresher and retains more nutrients. Local Harvest's goal is to have 50 percent of their products come from within 150 miles of St. Louis. Local Harvest, a recent *Riverfront Times* Best Grocery Store winner, works with regional farmers who practice sustainable agricultural methods that promote a sound environment and conserve energy.

Local Harvest's regional farmers and producers include lamb from Prairie Grass Farms, mushrooms from Ozark Forest, baked goods from Black Bear Bakery, Goshen Coffee, and much, much more. It's a great place to teach the kids or better yet learn for yourself more about how your food is grown. It's also an essential resource for those mornings when you sleep through the local farmers market and would like a locally roasted cup of coffee.

Top: A number of businesses have made Morgan Ford a destination. Photos by Bill Michalski; postcard by Big Small Town Designs, LLC.

Bottom: The Amsterdam Tavern is one of many watering holes that gives Morgan Ford its distinctive nightlife.

like a living organism—parts can be well when other parts are sick or injured.

In many ways, Morgan Ford has always been the counterweight to Grand. Though both have been primarily commercial for most of their lives, their life phases have come almost at exactly opposite times. When Grand has been up or on the rise, Morgan Ford has been down. Because of their adjacent communities, Grand has usually been the more affluent of the two and has usually been able to weather periods of decline better. However, as suburbanization took its toll on Tower Grove Heights and Tower Grove East in the 1960s and 1970s, Morgan Ford and the Oak Hill neighborhood were better able to adapt because it was more of a working-class community.

But as Tower Grove Heights recovered in the 1980s and 1990s, Morgan Ford and Oak Hill languished. Morgan Ford had been disfigured by the introduction of a number of noncompatible uses over the years, and even low rents could not attract the same kind of activity that was taking place on Grand. Exacerbating the situation even more was that a viaduct over railroad tracks to south on Morgan Ford was out for a number of years during the 1990s and the beginning of the twenty-first century. This drastically reduced automotive traffic in the district.

However, things drastically changed after 1999 when the viaduct reopened. As housing prices along Grand escalated, many singles and couples looked west in the Oak Hill section of Tower Grove South for better housing deals. Consequently, Morgan Ford started to be seen as a gathering place for a younger crowd than what was now the norm on Grand. Younger-oriented eateries started springing up, augmented by hip antique shops and alternative health grocery stores—the kind of thing that you would see in many college towns.

ARSENAL

While not as associated with the Tower Grove community as Grand, Arsenal also runs through the heart of the neighborhood and is a major reference point. Indeed, if the neighborhood had a public square, it would be located at the intersection of Grand and Arsenal. The name of this important thoroughfare refers to an army facility built on the banks of the Mississippi in 1827. Because the Grand viaduct over Mill Creek Valley (just north of Chouteau) was not completed until 1882, most early visitors approached Tower Grove Park from Arsenal. Even after the viaduct was completed, the first streetcars came into the neighborhood along Arsenal, and the construction on Arsenal was a direct result of the streetcar. Even though it fronts the park, developers for the most part did not build large, single-family homes on the street because of streetcar noise. The few single-family homes built on the street were constructed for the most part before the late 1890s and the advent of the streetcar. Nonetheless, even though the street does not contain a lot of larger residences, it still has some of the most architecturally interesting homes of the community.

Since the streetcar's demise, Arsenal remains a busy thoroughfare, carrying thousands of automobiles through the neighborhood every day and permitting their passengers a close-up view of the magic and beauty of Tower Grove Park.

Top: One of the attractions of Arsenal is the range of architectural styles.

Bottom: MoKaBe's Coffeehouse (3606 Arsenal), run by three lesbian women is a popular destination for both gays and straights.

HARTFORD

Though not as well known as the major thoroughfares through the neighborhood, Hartford Street is perhaps one of Tower Grove's most representative streets. Home to both relatively well-off and relatively poor, white and black, straight and gay, and native and immigrant families, Hartford captures the diversity of the Tower Grove experience. Platted in the 1880s as one of the original streets of the Tower Grove Heights subdivision, Hartford's evolution closely mirrors that of the community.

Named after the home city of the Connecticut Mutual Life Insurance Company, the initial developer of the subdivision, Hartford developed slowly at first. A few Queen Anne homes were built in the early 1890s, and there was a bakery at the corner of Grand and Hartford with a handful of multifamily residences just to the west (built with the hope of taking advantage of the new streetcar). But for the most part, development languished.

However, after the World's Fair a new developer arrived to re-plat the lots and develop new deed restrictions. While they did not affect existing properties; these deed restrictions limited Hartford to residential uses, specified that the homes had to be single family (to take advantage of the proximity of the park), required that they be at least two stories and constructed of brick or stone, and stated that they had to sell for at least thirty-five hundred dollars. But it was the new realty company's mass marketing effort that set things off in Tower Grove Heights. Not only did the Connecticut Realty Company advertise extensively, but it also offered long-term financing—a new innovation in the American real estate industry—to potential buyers.

Yet on Hartford itself, the key event was the arrival of two big local builders, John Zimmerman and William Gilmore. Believing that the neighborhood was "hot" and that they could make a sub-stantial profit on the two streets that were deed-restricted single

3648 Hartford

DEED RESTRICTIONS

- Permits "necessary" outhouses or stables
- Requires 20 foot setback
- Has to be used as private dwelling
- Must be made out of brick or stone
- Must be 2 or more stories
- Dwelling must cost at least $3,500
- Prohibits business on site
- Must be single family
- Prohibits "nuisances"

family—Hartford and Juniata— in 1905 and 1906 Zimmerman and Gilmore built tracks of housing on these streets on "spec." Using standard building plans and materials popular at the time, they built these houses as a unit in a span of just a few months. A look at the 1910 census for the 3600/3700 block of Hartford gives some idea of who these first residents were. Most were native born; however, barely half were originally from Missouri. Most of the heads of household were in their late thirties or early forties and were either entrepreneurs or professionals. Most of the residents were homeowners, but a surprising number did not have a mortgage. Also, a number of households had servants. For the most part then, Hartford Street was a fairly prosperous place to live up until the Great Depression. In many ways, it was like any number of upper-middle-class suburban communities today.

Even with the Depression and World War II, Hartford probably did not change a great deal. From all indications, the community remained relatively prosperous. Pius V, for example, undertook a major beautification project in the 1930s that involved installing mosaics in the sanctuary. But as neighborhoods like Tower Grove lost their luster in the 1950s and 1960s with the rise of middle-class suburbs, Hartford became rather "rough," especially just west of Grand. However, that process reversed itself in the 1980s and 1990s as the neighborhood underwent another stage of transition. With its strong stock of large, single-family houses, Hartford east of Gustine became one of the first streets in Tower Grove to experience a resurgence in the 1980s. Interestingly, Hartford west of Gustine is now one of the hot addresses in Oak Hill as this part of Tower Grove goes through its renaissance.

Unlike much of Tower Grove Heights, which was developed by a number of small contractors, most of Hartford and Juniata were built out by two large developers—John Zimmerman and William Gilmore. The three houses shown were part of a line of nine "spec" houses that were built on the south side of the street in June 1905. Notice how close the houses on the left and right are to each other.

Hartford Coffee Company (3974 Hartford) is a pleasant neighborhood gathering place. University students often study here using the wireless Internet connection. Hartford offers kid-friendly snacks including Animal Crackers, Gold Fish, and Cheerios by the cup. They also roast their own beans twice a week, sometimes giving them local names like "Red Bird Blend" in honor, of course, of the beloved baseball Cardinals. The *Riverfront Times* in 2006 recognized Hartford Coffee Company as its Best Coffee House.

UTAH

Like Arsenal, Utah originated as one of the borders of the army arsenal constructed on the Mississippi River, and it would eventually extend to Morgan Ford on the west. While it transects much of St. Louis's South Side, Utah has always been the most distinguished street in Tower Grove. This is largely because of Utah Place, a boulevard featuring canopied medians and large, stately homes.

Constructed between 1905 and 1920, Utah Place features some of the most distinguished residences in the city of St. Louis. Required by the original deed restrictions to be individually designed by an architect and to sell for at least $14,000 ($400,000–$500,000 in today's dollars), homes on Utah are not only some of the largest houses in the city, but also they are some of the most architecturally striking. While most of the houses were constructed in some variation of a Victorian motif, some utilize Romanesque and Italianate styles. Even the two-family structures in the block between Spring and Gustine are some of most architecturally significant multifamily buildings in the city.

Because of the homes' stature, Utah Place was one of the most desirable addresses in St. Louis before World War II. In fact, locals often referred to it as "millionaires row." However, because of changing styles and trends, Utah may have been one of the first streets to show early signs of aging. Though spectacular in scale, Utah houses did not possess many new housing features that were being introduced at the time—like air conditioning. As a result, even residents who had the most spacious addresses between Grand and Spring began migrating to the suburbs shortly after the war to take advantage of larger lots and newer amenities. Oftentimes, these residents were replaced with groups as opposed to families. Being as large as they are, they became perfect homes for religious orders and similar groups. Even Utah's medians were transformed. But if Utah Place was one of the first streets to decline in the late 1950s and early 1960s, it was one of the first ones to undergo gentrification in the 1980s. With their spacious interiors and architectural detail, Utah homes—both single- and two-family—became a magnet for young urban professionals.

Although never having the panache of Utah Place, Utah Street west of Gustine has a very interesting character that speaks volumes for the diversity of both Utah and Tower Grove. Once it crosses Gustine and the western border of Tower Grove Heights, Utah travels down a steep hill into the original Oak Hill neighborhood. As it moves down the hill approaching Roger Place, Utah is flanked by mostly two-family residences built roughly at the same time as the larger structures to the east. But once it crosses Roger Place, Utah is lined for the next four blocks with small single-family houses built in the 1920s. Though modest in comparison to the magnificent structures along Utah Place, these homes were the foundation of a stable working-class community that allowed the neighborhood to prevail over the challenges of the 1960s and 1970s.

A Utah Place home.

HALLIDAY

Halliday Street runs from Michigan Avenue on the east to Grand on the west, wholly inside Tower Grove East. Although only five blocks long, Halliday was originally part of two different subdivisions. The section west of Louisiana, composed of mostly single-family homes, was part of the original Tower Grove Heights subdivision. The section to the east was built out with primarily two-family flats; it was initially held by Joseph Charless, Jr., son of one of St. Louis's earliest dignitaries. Eventually, a group of German speculators known as the Arsenal and Tower Grove Improvement Company purchased the Charless land. They renamed the tract "Wilhelm's Hohe."

Both ends of Halliday tell not only interesting stories about the street but also about Tower Grove and turn-of-the-century St. Louis. The western end demonstrates both turn-of-the-century home styles and the importance of the 1904 World's Fair in pushing development both before and after the Fair. Unlike the section of Tower Grove Heights that was west of Grand and south of Arsenal, most of the homes on Halliday were constructed shortly before the Fair opened while the land was still held by the life insurance company. In an advertisement for two homes in the 3500 block of Halliday that appeared in the *St. Louis Post-Dispatch*, the houses are favorably compared to more expensive houses being built at roughly the same time in

HALLIDAY AVE.
3500-3538
- Second floors are "simply grand"
  - Mantels "finer than in many $15,000 or $20,000 homes"
  - Hardwood floors of beech
- Attics finished
- Bathrooms large
  - Plumbing brass nickel-plated and "strictly sanitary"
  - Porcelain bathtub
  - Italian marble washstand
  - "Noiseless water closet"
  - Tile floor vitreous

Halliday is one of the most attractive streets in the neighborhood due to both the quality of its architecture, as well as the lushness of its tree canopy. At top are houses from the ad on the previous page.

the Central West End, and mention is made of the many amenities that "will be featured at the World's Fair." While the western end of Halliday reflects market trends affecting single-family construction immediately after the turn of the century, the rental property at the eastern end reflects a similar transformation taking place in multifamily construction. Until this time, most residential properties—even multifamily ones—were built by small builders to a buyer's specifications. However, the two-family structures in the "Wilhelm's Hohe" section of Halliday were built according to a standard floor plan for mass marketing.

The life of Halliday, after its initial build out, essentially dove-tailed that of the rest of Tower Grove East and the Tower Grove community. Both the single-family and multifamily ends of the street went through a Golden Age in the 1910s and 1920s, followed by a period of decline in the 1930s. But for the most part, the real transformation of the street did not occur until the 1950s and 1960s. Like similar streets such as Crittenden and Pestalozzi, the more affluent west end started its slide earlier than the rental section to the east. And like the western half of the original Tower Grove Heights, the single-family portion of Halliday began its resurgence earlier than the portion east of Louisiana. However, both halves have become very desirable places to live. With one of the most luscious street canopies in St. Louis and in easy walking distance to the front entrance to Tower Grove Park, Halliday residents see it as a hidden jewel on the city's South Side.

Messiah Lutheran photographed from Tower Grove Park.

Chapter 5

LANDMARKS AND INSTITUTIONS

Whenever one thinks of a community, images of important places or buildings come to mind. These places can be public spaces like fountains or squares. They can be private spaces such as major commercial buildings or districts. But they can also be institutional spaces—churches and schools, for example. Whether they are public, private, or institutional, these spaces define a community. They provide not only an identity for outsiders but also for the inhabitants of the community.

Tower Grove is blessed with landmarks that give the neighborhood a powerful sense of place. Obviously, the park and South Grand are important places in Tower Grove. However, there are a host of others that give the community an identity like no other in St. Louis. Although no two people may ever come up with the same list of landmarks, the following are some of the important places that have defined Tower Grove over time.

SOUTH GRAND MEDIANS

In the 1990s, traffic on South Grand moved at a frantic pace. There were accidents and many near misses resulting in a call to action from the community to bring about traffic-calming measures.

In 1997, a neighborhood effort to slow traffic and replace crumbling concrete medians with well-watered, greener medians began at the suggestion of Anne Moore, a Tower Grove East resident. Representatives of five adjacent neighborhood organizations, two Grand Boulevard business associations, two associations of supporters of Tower Grove Park and Compton Hill Reservoir Park and civic betterment associations including Gateway Greening, Operation Brightside, and Arts in Transit met and formed a committee. After two years of presentations to neighbors and the city, with the help of Parsons Brinckerhoff and TSI Engineering, the committee put together a winning $1.5 million federal grant proposal.

Completed in 2004, the South Grand medians include traffic-calming devices known as "bump outs," a new median with automatic sprinklers to water plants and flowers, a bicycle lane, new historic-style lights designed to match those in Tower Grove Park, and wider sidewalk corners at about thirteen side streets.

PELICAN BUILDING

Built in 1895 for beer baron Anton Griesedieck, Pelican's Grill was billed during the 1904 World's Fair as a "first class restaurant and liquortorium." Also known for a time as Edmund Popp's, the building became know as the Pelican for owners James and Catherine Pelican, who ran the restaurant by that same name from 1945 to 1978. The Pelican Restaurant was well known for their turtle soup.

CARPENTER LIBRARY

Carpenter Library is located in the Tower Grove South neighborhood on Grand Boulevard between Utah Place and McDonald Avenue and is the city's most-used library. This St. Louis Public Library branch was named after George Oliver Carpenter, who donated the land for the branch in 1925. George Carpenter was the vice president and general manager of the National Lead Co. in St. Louis. He was also a president of the board of directors of the St. Louis Public Library and was a member of the board of directors of Washington University.

The original library building, designed by the architectural firm of Trueblood and Graf, was completed in 1926. Carpenter Library was renovated extensively in the last decade, providing twice the floor space of the original 1927 building. The library offers special English-as-a-second-language collections, including substantial materials in Vietnamese, Chinese, and Serbo-Croatian languages.

DICKMANN BUILDING

The Dickmann Building is the second structure at this site, replacing a two-story building dating to the early 1900s. Constructed by the real estate company of future St. Louis mayor Bernard Dickmann in 1926, the Dickmann Building is a Gothic Revival of white glazed terra cotta, designed by Wedemeyer and Nelson. Its six-story height, nearly twice that of anything else in the Grand commercial strip, was a bold statement of confidence in the future of the neighborhood.

For a time, Bernard Dickmann's building featured a German restaurant on the street level as well as a beer garden on the rooftop. Thus, the building's elevator went all the way to the rooftop. This was unusual for the time, and passersby will notice the top floor penthouse looks like two stories.

Bernard Dickmann sold the building to the Jesuits, who published the *Queen's Work*—a well-known Catholic publication—there until the mid-1970s when the Liguori purchased the *Queen's Work* and other Jesuit publications. The current building owner purchased the Dickmann Building in 1980 and continues to receive inquiries from former *Queen's Work* employees as well as mail still addressed to the publication at its former South Grand address.

The two buildings flanking the Dickmann Building—the Woolworth Building to the south and the Butler Building north across the alley—are connected to the Dickmann Building via tunnels under the alley. Local folklore notes the possibility of a speakeasy on the second floor of the Woolworth Building during Prohibition.

The Dickmann Building (3115 South Grand Boulevard)

From 1999 to 2005, a complete renovation of the building was completed, following the guidelines required by the Missouri State Historic Tax Credits and the National Register of Historic Places. The Dickmann Building was added to the National Register in 1999.

CORNER OF GRAND AND ARSENAL

B uilt in 1909, the building at the corner of Grand and Arsenal housed the Arsenal Movie Theatre along with several other small businesses. The theatre closed with the advent of "Talking Pictures."

The second floor housed medical offices for more than fifty years for a father and son, both Dr. Heinecke. The senior Dr. Heinecke was a medical doctor while the younger Dr. Heinecke was a dentist.

The current owner is working hard to maintain the building's original "round top" style windows form. This type of restoration is often cost prohibitive, as this window style is no longer mass produced. These kinds of rehabilitation issues are often solved, or assisted by, historic tax credits.

3101 South Grand Boulevard today.

STANDARD OIL GAS STATION

Built during World War I, the BP station at 3182 South Grand is one of the few remaining examples of gasoline stations from that period. It has survived in some semblance of its original form due to the preservation-mindedness of the neighborhood residents.

Strassberger's Conservatory, (2300 South Grand Boulevard) served South St. Louis's growing German immigrant population.

THE STRASSBERGER BUILDING

Strassberger's Conservatory served South St. Louis's growing German immigrant population. Built by Clemens Strassberger and completed in 1906, the Strassberger Conservatory was part of an effort to preserve the German traditions of singing societies, bands, orchestras, and other musical societies.

Designed by St. Louis Architect Otto J Wilhemi, the conservatory offered lessons in deportment considered essential to immigrant assimilation into St. Louis high society.

After the Conservatory closed in the late 1930s, the building had many uses. Placed on the National Register of Historic Places in 1980, the building was converted into retail spaces at the street level and loft apartments above.

THE REHABBER'S CLUB

Established in 2000 for folks interested in rehabbing in the city of St. Louis, the first meeting was organized by then local realtor Marti Frumhoff and held at MoKaBe's Coffee House on Arsenal. Meetings today include rehab camaraderie, a lecture, a workshop, or perhaps a walking tour of buildings under renovation in one of St. Louis's historic neighborhoods. Meetings are held the third Saturday of the month from 9:30 a.m. to 11:30 a.m.

Frumhoff passed away suddenly in May 2007. In honor of her life and work the Marti Frumhoff Memorial Garden was built at the triangle wedge at Utah and Morgan Ford, along the edge of the burgeoning Morgan Ford Business District.

THE CAPISTRANO

Another "neighborhood institution," Susie Gudermuth has been called a therapist for buildings down on their luck. Since coming from University City to Tower Grove Heights in 1980 Susie has been behind the rehabilitation of more than thirty buildings in the area. The Capistrano apartment building is one of her most notable renovations. The Capistrano, once empty and dilapidated, has been returned to life as condominiums. The building's name is probably linked to Mission San Juan Capistrano in Southern California. According to Gudermuth, there are photos of the builder Zeppenfeld's family touring San Juan Capistrano.

3905 Utah Street

DIVINE SCIENCE CHRISTIAN CHURCH

3716 Wyoming Street

Founded by the Reverend Henry Schroeder, this group started meeting in 1892 at Broadway and Shenandoah under the name German Society of Divine Science. In 1898, they incorporated as the Society of Practical Christianity and purchased the church at 18th and Pestalozzi streets. In 1915, the cornerstone of a new church was laid at 3617 Wyoming.

Although known as the Church of Practical Christianity, the congregation officially changed its name to First Divine Science Church of St. Louis in 1928.

Residents of Tower Grove Heights Neighborhood Association have met here on the fourth Tuesday of every other month for more than twenty years.

ST. PIUS V

Ground was broken for St. Pius V Catholic Church (3310 South Grand Boulevard) in 1916. Its architecture was the Romanesque and "sturdy" Baroque style of the sixteenth century. It was constructed of sandstone, and by the 1950s, it was so weatherworn that it was replaced with Indiana limestone, giving the edifice a slimmer look. Its stained glass windows were the work of Emil Frei, famed art glass and mosaic designer whose classic and unique glass window creations adorn churches worldwide. Emil Frei was also the co-owner of Ravenna Mosaics, which was commissioned to do the mosaics in the New Cathedral on Lindell Boulevard. Emil Frei's art glass studios were located on South Grand until 1972.

St. Pius V had humble beginnings as an Irish immigrant church but by World War II had grown to be one of the largest, most prestigious parishes in the Archdiocese of St. Louis. The church nave's ornate mosaic representation of Christ the King—completed in the fall of 1937 during the Depression—is a testament to this. The post-war baby boom swelled its membership and school enrollment and prompted expansion and improvements of the church and grounds by the mid-1950s.

By the 1970s, South St. Louis's ethnic makeup

Church interior, 1937.

was beginning to change again as middle-class whites fled for the suburbs. African Americans and Asian and African immigrants and refugees took their place in the 1980s. The dramatic demographic shift during the 1980s and 1990s created social tension and demanded a response. In the 1990s, parishioners were mobilized to advocate for social change, a value still held today.

If St. Pius's members are fewer today, they are more diverse—a mix of old, young, refugee, immigrant, longtime neighborhood residents, and suburbanites. In the 1990s, the 10 a.m. liturgy became more vital with warmer hospitality, livelier music, and more dynamic preaching. St. Pius's ministries to the elderly, homebound, immigrant, and poor grew. Parish finances were stabilized; stewardship was emphasized.

In 2003, St. Pius took the painful step of closing its school and merging with another to form St. Frances Cabrini Academy. In late 2004, St. Pius learned it would close as part of a realignment of South Side parishes. The parish strenuously defended its viability and purpose, and the archbishop allowed it to remain open.

HOLY FAMILY

The Reverend J. F. Reuther organized Holy Family Parish, at 4125 Humphrey Street, in 1898. The Tower Grove Park area was rapidly becoming a more developed neighborhood and the new parish was to serve the needs of its German-speaking people. Holy Family at one time had a large grade school and many organizations that played significant roles in the history of South St. Louis.

The first mass was celebrated on November 10, 1898, in a rented home on Wyoming Street. The home's first floor was fitted up as a chapel. The parish school began its work in the chapel rooms in January 1899.

The church site on the northwest corner of Humphrey Street and Oak Hill Avenue was purchased and construction began on the 125 × 350 foot lot in 1899. The church was dedicated on November 28, 1899, with final completion and erection of a sister's home accomplished in 1907.

Parish growth made necessary the building of a four-room school addition and auditorium in 1912. Cornerstone laying ceremonies for the present church occurred on November 22, 1926.

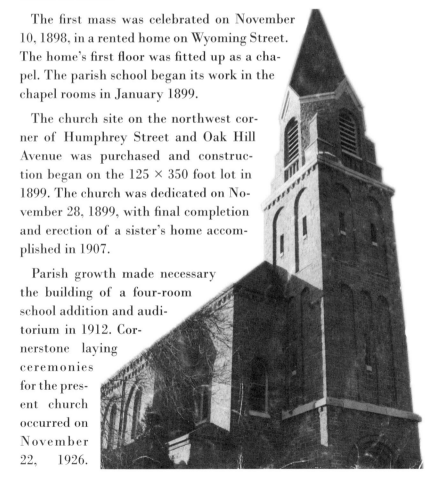

Archbishop Glennon dedicated the new building on June 19, 1927. It was designed in the Gothic and Romanesque style by Ludwig and Dreisoerner and is constructed of variegated Missouri red granite with a massive appearance. The brick arch spanning the sanctuary is among the widest of its kind. The present school at 4132 Wyoming was completed in 1941, followed by the convent at 4161 Humphrey in 1956, and a parish center building at 4141 Humphrey in 1963.

Holy Family Parish was an anchor in the Oak Hill community through 2005. As the Catholic population of South St. Louis declined, it became necessary to reduce the number of parishes. In 2005, the parish of Holy Family was suppressed, and the parishioners were invited to become part of St. Pius V Parish. Today, the former parish building has found new life as the headquarters of Cfx, a visual communications company. With a nod to the past, the company kept the still-working pipe organ. A time-lapse, panoramic tour of the renovation and transformation of the building can be found on Cfx's website.

MESSIAH LUTHERAN

3716 Wyoming Street

Messiah's steeple is one of the most distinguished architectural features in Tower Grove.

Messiah Lutheran Church traces its roots back to meetings held in December 1907 when local parishioners began talking about the logistics of starting a congregation. Services began in January 1908 and were conducted in German but eventually alternated weekly between German and English. Kleekamps' Hall on Grand Boulevard was Messiah's first location, secured at the cost of just five dollars per Sunday.

The Reverend William Wilk was Messiah's first pastor. The South Grand location was dedicated in December of 1929. One of the local newspapers at the time called the church a "symphony of charm and beauty."

During the 1960s and early 1970s, however, many young families moved to the suburbs, and Messiah, along with countless other urban churches, had to redefine itself in a changing neighborhood.

No longer serving a primarily German area, Messiah shifted its focus to be a church for the people of all nations. They host events that try to bring in school and neighborhood children, such as "Light up the Night," their annual evening of fun and food on Halloween. Messiah is further visible in the neighborhood by caroling at Christmas, hosting the Messiah Pumpkin Patch, and taking part in the Grand/South Grand Area House Tour. In September of 2008, the church celebrated its one hundredth anniversary.

ST. JOHN'S EPISCOPAL

Founded on St. John's Day (December 28) 1841, St. John's Episcopal Church, St. Louis, is the second-oldest Episcopal parish in St. Louis and the fifth oldest in the state of Missouri.

St. John's relocated to Tower Grove from Lafayette Square after the Tornado of 1896 destroyed the steeple of the church as well as many parishioners' homes. The present Tudor and Gothic stone structure at 3664 Arsenal Street almost duplicates the design of its predecessor in Lafayette Square.

St. John's has been the home to the Wainwright Family (of the Wainwright Brewery and Wainwright Building fame) and Betty Grable, known as the #1 Pin-up Girl of World War II and an American icon, was baptized as an infant in the baptismal font situated in the front of the nave. St. John's first rector, Whiting Griswold, is great grandfather to Frank Griswold, the twenty-fifth presiding bishop of the Episcopal Church from January 1998 until November 2006.

The interior architectural style is an "upside down ship's hull." Visitors will also notice on the pews rectangular areas where brass

numbers once were attached, which denote where certain people and families sat, a reminder of the "pew rental" system. St. John's was one of the first Episcopal churches in Missouri to discontinue this practice of "caste separation."

OAK HILL PRESBYTERIAN

Oak Hill Presbyterian Church began in a frame church building at the corner of Bent Avenue and Humphrey Street in 1895. Mrs. Lucy Bent Russell donated this original lot.

On March 17, 1907, the frame church was destroyed in a fire, and in the following summer, the first lot at the present site at Oak Hill Avenue and Connecticut Street was purchased. For some months after the fire, services were held in a lodge hall at Morgan Ford and Connecticut. Later, a tent was raised for summer services on the new lot, but during cold weather, the congregation worshipped in a hall at Morgan Ford and Juniata.

The first building to be occupied at the Oak Hill Avenue site was a chapel, which was completed in September 1911. Dedication of the present church building took place on June 20, 1920, and in the following year the manse was acquired.

In October 1954, a new educational building, joining the church to an adjacent annex, was dedicated. During the summer of 1969, the church sanctuary was renovated at a cost of fifty-five thousand dollars. In 1943, Oak Hill Church sponsored the organization of the First Presbyterian Church of Affton as a mission.

TOWER GROVE ABBEY

Tower Grove Abbey, at 2336 Tennessee Avenue, was originally built as the "German Evangelical Saint Lukas Church of St. Louis." The cornerstone was laid in 1906, with a total construction cost of twelve thousand dollars.

This beautiful century-old church today is a successful multi-use performance center for arts, education, and community programs and for two churches. Now home to Stray Dog Theatre, this acoustically superb structure seats 150 guests. Magnificent architecture and stained glass windows await visitors.

Stray Dog Theatre started as a tenant in the handsome Tower Grove Abbey. The building had long fascinated Stray Dog Artistic Director Gary Bell, who lived next door in what was once St. Luke's parsonage. Bell suspected that the old church had dramatic possibilities. When representatives of the church that owned the building dropped by to suggest a shared arrangement, Stray Dog bit and bought the building.

Today, Tower Grove Abbey is a community center in addition to a theatre. The congregations that worship there continue to do so, although the pipe organ has been donated to the Compton Heights Concert Band. Ballet and yoga classes meet at the Abbey, as does the Tower Grove East neighborhood association. Stray Dog Theatre continues to build on its solid theatrical reputation. Their productions regularly garner Kevin Kline Award nominations and awards in recognition of outstanding achievement in professional theatre in the greater St. Louis area.

ST. ELIZABETH ACADEMY

The German-speaking Sisters of the Most Precious Blood immigrated to America in 1873 after being expelled from Germany and Bismark's newly formed German Empire.

In 1882, the Sisters founded St. Elizabeth Academy in the Schiller home at Arsenal and Grand as a boarding school for girls. Initially a two-year program, the original curriculum included the finishing school subjects of music, art embroidery, languages, and religious education, with practical training in domestic subjects added later. At that time, cooking, sewing, and nutrition were considered professional training.

As office work became an acceptable occupation for women, typing and stenography were added in the 1890s. By 1892, a four-year college preparatory curriculum was in place. The original building facing Crittenden Street on Elizabeth Avenue was completed in 1894. At the wishes of its original patron Mrs. Schiller, St. Elizabeth took in orphans. Instruction in the nineteenth century was in German.

St. Elizabeth Academy (main entrance currently at 3401 Arsenal Street) remains a vibrant keystone of Tower Grove. The school celebrated its 125th anniversary in 2007 and continues its mission of "Developing the successful woman inside each girl" in its second century.

HORACE MANN SCHOOL

Built in 1901, Mann School (4047 Juniata) is one of architect William Ittner's early elementary schools showing his pioneering "open plan," which emphasized light and air in both halls and classrooms. Ittner's open-plan design would revolutionize school architecture in the United States. The division of the interior spaces clearly articulated on the exterior are enhanced by a set of Tudor elements. His imaginative use of siting and structure ornamentation resulted in a distinct style and identity for each of his buildings.

William Ittner was associated with the St. Louis Board of Education between 1897 and 1914. He wrote extensively about his design theories, which made St. Louis Public Schools a leader, design-wise, nationwide.

Mann School was added to the National Register of Historic Places in 1992. 2009 Status: Recommended for closure; faces possible demolition for the construction of a new South Side school.

ROOSEVELT HIGH SCHOOL

Roosevelt High School (3230 Hartford Avenue) was built in 1925 on what was once Picker Cemetery. Designed by Rockwell Milligan, the architectural style of the school building is English Renaissance of the transition of the Tudor and Elizabethan periods. The builder was E. C. Gerbard Building Company. Total cost of construction was $1,611,100.48.

Named after President Theodore Roosevelt, their mascot is The Rough Riders, in recognition of the namesake and his unit from the Spanish-American War. Bwana, the name of Roosevelt's yearbook,

means literally "Great Chief." When Teddy Roosevelt was on an expedition in Africa, the natives referred to him as a great chief because of his great skills and courage. The first Bwana was published in June 1925, and the traditional yearbook and its name continues today.

In 1997, Roosevelt underwent a $10 million renovation, which uncovered a long hidden mosaic ceiling in the auditorium.

In 2009, the Roosevelt High School Junior ROTC Color Guard and Drill Team had the honor of marching in President Obama's Inaugural Parade. Out of fourteen hundred marching units who applied nationwide just forty were accepted.

Because of its former use as a cemetery, some say the school is haunted. Bones once surfaced to the top of the football field, and one of the graves collapsed on the front lawn, which had to be immediately filled in.

SHENANDOAH SCHOOL

The school is a remarkable building, known widely for the braided limestone columns at its entrance. Designed by Rockwell Milligan and built in 1925, Shenandoah School (3412 Shenandoah Avenue) is an excellent example of the eclectic strain in 1920s American architecture. Combining Spanish Revival and Renaissance Revival elements on an imposing buff-brick body with a red tile roof, Shenandoah is an architectural neighborhood treasure.

LUSTRON HOMES

L ustron homes are porcelain-paneled dwellings that were touted as miracle houses and were the answer to the postwar housing shortage. They were maintenance-free, according to their manufacturer, the Lustron Corp. of Ohio—though they might need to be hosed off occasionally.

Between 1947 and 1950, more than twenty-four hundred Lustron homes were built throughout the eastern United States, often in small clusters. Their selling price ranged from seven thousand to ten thousand dollars. More than three thousand parts went into one home, which took about 350 man hours to build. If things went well, the exterior of a Lustron home could be assembled in one day, although the installation of cabinets and other interior finishing could take another week or two.

Almost always built on a concrete slab, Lustron homes also could claim to be rat proof, termite proof, and fireproof. Inside, they were efficient, with a number of space-saving designs that included pocket doors that slid back into the walls, built-in dressing tables in the bedroom, and closets with sliding doors throughout. The homes also featured radiant heating from the ceiling; unfortunately this was a major design flaw in many occupants' eyes. Another innovative design was a unique machine that could wash both clothes and dishes, although not at the same time.

The Lustron house was the brainchild of Carl Strandlund, who manufactured porcelain-coated steel panels that had been used for gas stations and fast food restaurants such as White Castle. He hit on the idea of using porcelain-coated steel panels for prefab houses. He even got government backing for his project because of the postwar housing shortage.

The Lustron movement faltered due to the company's inability to mass produce enough houses fast enough to satisfy the demand.

One of two excellent examples at 4122 and 4123 McDonald Avenue.

Local historians have noted the significance of the Lustron homes because of the unique design and because they are a reflection of the American belief in the use technology to solve problems.

FRIENDLY'S

Friendly's was established 1928. Initially a social club, today Friendly's is an authentic "old school" South Side eating and drinking establishment known for its fried chicken and reasonable prices. Although it is just south of the parameters set in this book, has served Tower Grove residents for generations.

BIBLIOGRAPHY

Cahn, William. *A Matter of Life and Death: The Connecticut Mutual Story*. New York: Random House, 1970.

Fox, Tim, ed. *Where We Live: A Guide to St. Louis Communities*. St. Louis: Missouri Historical Society, 1995.

Hannon, Robert E., ed. *St. Louis: Its Neighborhoods and Neighbors, Landmarks and Milestones*. St. Louis: St. Louis Regional Planning and Growth Association, 1986.

Magnan, William B. and Marcella C. *The Streets of St. Louis: A History of St. Louis Street Names*. St. Louis: Virginia Publishing, 1996.

Primm, James Neal. *Lion of the Valley: St. Louis, Missouri*, 2d ed. Boulder, Colo.: Pruett Publishing Company, 1990.

Sandweiss, Eric. *St. Louis: The Evolution of an American Urban Landscape*. Philadelphia: Temple University Press, 2001.

Southwestern Mercantile Association. *Southwest Saint Louis: Its Mercantile Interests and Prominent Citizens*. St. Louis: Southwestern Mercantile Association, 1908.

Teaford, Jon C. *The Twentieth-Century American City*, 2d ed. Baltimore: The John Hopkins University Press, 1993.

Toft, Carolyn Hewes, with Lynn Josse. *St. Louis: Landmarks and Historical Districts*. St. Louis: Landmarks Association of St. Louis, Inc., 2002.

Von Hoffman, Alexander. *Local Attachments: The Making of an American Urban Neighborhood, 1850–1920*. Baltimore: The John Hopkins University Press, 1994.

Wayman, Norbury L. *History of St. Louis Neighborhoods: Grand-Oak Hill*. St. Louis: St. Louis Community Development Agency, 1981.

Issues of the *Grand Oak Hill Community Development Corporation Newsletter*, the *T.G.E news*, and the *Tower Grove Heights Gazette*.

Minutes of the monthly meetings of the Grand Oak Hill Community Development Corporation, the Tower Grove East Neighborhood Association, and the Tower Grove Heights Neighborhood Association.